A Perceforest Reader

Also translated by Nigel Bryant

The High Book of the Grail:
A Translation of the thirteenth-century romance of *Perlesvaus*

Chrétien de Troyes, *Perceval: The Story of the Grail*

Robert de Boron, *Merlin and the Grail*

The Legend of the Grail

Perceforest: The Prehistory of King Arthur's Britain

The True Chronicles of Jean le Bel 1290-1360

A Perceforest Reader

Selected episodes from
Perceforest: The Prehistory of King Arthur's Britain

TRANSLATED BY NIGEL BRYANT

D. S. BREWER

First published 2011
D. S. Brewer, Cambridge

ISBN 978 1 84384 290 3

D. S. Brewer is an imprint of Boydell & Brewer Ltd
PO Box 9, Woodbridge, Suffolk, IP12 3DF, UK
and of Boydell & Brewer Inc.
668 Mount Hope Ave, Rochester, NY 14620-2731, USA
website: www.boydellandbrewer.com

The publisher has no responsibility for the continued existence or
accuracy of URLs for external or third-party internet websites referred
to in this book, and does not guarantee that any content on such
websites is, or will remain, accurate or appropriate.

A CIP catalogue record for this book is available
from the British Library

Contents

undertakes a mysterious mission; it leads him to encounter the
enchanter Aroés, who has set himself up as God of the Sheer
Mountain.

The author of Perceforest sends his knights out to confront a
world of awesome marvels. The complexity of the created world,
and the author's fascination with it, are nowhere expressed as
startlingly as in an adventure encountered by King Perceforest's
son when he's stranded on a distant island.

Perceforest has been described as 'a mine of folkloric motifs',
and is famous for featuring this, the first written version of the
story that has come to be known as 'the Sleeping Beauty'.

One of the most striking characters in the later books of Perceforest is Passelion, destined to be an ancestor of no less a figure
than Merlin.

The author of Perceforest draws material from many sources,
linking his prehistory of Arthurian Britain to numerous existing
traditions and histories. In this episode, he makes the murder of
Julius Caesar an act of revenge for his destruction of Britain.

Britain, recovering from its destruction by the Romans, needs
a new king and queen. The destined ones are Gallafur and 'the
Maiden of the Dragons'. They are descendants not only of Perceforest and Gadifer but of Alexander, too, and their bloodline is
to continue to King Arthur himself. Arthur will thus have Greek
blood, inherited from Alexander the Great. But, although the
Maiden of the Dragons has captured Gallafur's heart, he will
not be worthy of her unless he first achieves the Adventure of the
Red Sword.

Introduction

The French romance of *Perceforest* is a work of exceptional richness and importance, creating a prehistory of King Arthur's Britain and an ancestry of all the major Arthurian figures – Arthur, Merlin, Lancelot and many more. But it is much more than a mere prelude to more familiar tales. It is a magnificent epic story in its own right, and offers a wealth of intriguing material to all medievalists – to historians as well as Arthurian enthusiasts: it has, indeed, been justly described as 'a veritable encyclopaedia of fourteenth-century chivalry' and 'a mine of folkloric motifs'.[1] But in the field of Arthurian literature it has been relatively little known, and the words 'encyclopaedia' and 'mine' may give a hint at the reason: another notable feature of *Perceforest* is its extraordinary length. It is composed of six books, each the length of a substantial novel – the shortest is as long as *Moby Dick*.

A complete account of this vast romance, including a full translation of all key passages, has now been made available by D. S. Brewer, first published in 2011. This 'Sampler' is a selection of episodes from that edition, and is intended as a simple introduction to the work, a work of such variety and imaginative scope that it would have been quite possible to assemble four or five compilations. The hope is that it gives a tempting indication of *Perceforest*'s wide range of tone – comic, tragic, realistic, fantastic – and of theme: in its exploration of ideas about love, magic, religion, women, kingship and the code of chivalry, *Perceforest* gives remarkable insights into the medieval mind.

Jacques Barchilon, L'histoire de la Belle au bois dormant dans le Perceforest', *Fabula* vol.31, issues 1-2 (1990), pp.17-23. The 'fourteenth-century' dating has been much debated: all the surviving manuscripts of *Perceforest* were produced after 1450, but there are a number of reasons to date its original composition to c.1330-40. See *Perceforest*, tr. Bryant (D.S.Brewer, 2011), Introduction, especially pp.24-5.

The Story

A complete synopsis of Perceforest's narratives would be unreadably dense. The anonymous author draws on many sources – the *Lancelot-Grail*, Alexander romances, Roman histories, medieval travel writing and oral tradition – as he interweaves and interconnects a vast number of episodes in a complex and intricately conceived way. To give a context for the selections in this Sampler, however, here is a broad outline of the story:

Setting his work in the chronicle tradition of Geoffrey of Monmouth's *History of the Kings of Britain*, the author begins by describing the arrival in Britain of refugees from Troy. But in time, a succession of weak rulers sees the land go into decline, leaving its people in urgent need of revitalisation, of new blood.

This comes when Alexander the Great and his Greek companions, sailing to the king of India's coronation, are caught in a storm and driven to Britain. Alexander establishes two of his protégés, Gadifer and Betis (who later earns the name 'Perceforest'), as brother-kings of England and Scotland. They find the forests infested by the 'evil clan' of Darnant the Enchanter, notable especially for their abuse of women, but in a series of stirring adventures Perceforest, Gadifer and their knights succeed in driving them out despite their use of sorcery as a weapon.

But then news of Alexander's death sends Perceforest into a deep depression, and at the same time his brother Gadifer is maimed while hunting a monstrous boar. With both kings incapable of providing leadership there are threats to both kingdoms – rebellion from within and invasion from without – but valiant English and Scottish knights succeed in repelling these attacks.

Gadifer remains crippled but Perceforest is roused from his inertia. He establishes a glorious chivalric civilisation in Britain, founding a knightly order that prefigures the Round Table of Arthur, and introduces a new 'Sovereign God' in place of the multiple gods of Perceforest's pagan past. His knights, often helped by Zephir, a guardian spirit of the most surprising and ambiguous kind, accomplish a series of wonderful adventures both in Britain and in the Low Countries (which may well have been the author's homeland), involving love, revenge and magic.

The kings' children are at the forefront of these adventures; but then Perceforest's eldest son becomes infatuated with a Roman girl, whose treachery enables Julius Caesar to launch an invasion in which Perceforest and all his forces are annihilated and the kingdom is utterly destroyed.

A third generation of knights and maidens restore the land, and one of Gadifer's grandsons, Ourseau, takes revenge on Caesar. Another of his grandsons, Gallafur, is destined to marry Alexander's granddaughter, 'the Maiden of the Dragons', to give Britain a new king and queen; their union is to begin a line leading to a king who will draw a sword which Gallafur has embedded in a great stone – King Arthur himself, who will thus be a descendant of none other than Alexander. But before that union can take place, Gallafur must first achieve heroic feats by accomplishing 'the Adventure of the Red Sword' and casting out the enchantments that still beset Britain.

And he cannot enjoy his success for long. The fragility of kingdoms is seen again as Britain is invaded for a second time: in a reversal of the Trojan War, the Sicambrians, a people of Trojan blood, attack and destroy the 'Greek' civilisation of Britain.

But Gallafur's son, rescued by Zephir, survives and learns of the coming of the 'New Law', and sees a holy vessel brought to Britain to await the knight who is to achieve the Grail quest. The kingdom of Arthur is soon to come.

How Perceforest earned his name

Newly crowned king of England by Alexander, Betis is warned repeatedly that the forests of the land are infested by an 'evil clan' headed by Darnant the Enchanter. Their most damning crimes are the offences they commit against women, and they are adept at using magic as a weapon. Betis is about to commission the building of a new castle on the site of the land's first tournament, but...

'My lord,' Nicorant replied, 'I'll do all you command except fetch timber from the forest! No workman would dare go there to cut or fell: he'd be lost in an instant, spirited away by the enchanters who dwell there!'

'Go and buy the stone, Nicorant,' said King Betis, 'and I'll see to the forest!'

A little later, Betis fell asleep after dinner in the warmth of the afternoon; and he dreamed that the dwarf who'd directed him to the place of his coronation appeared before him and said:

'Cowardly king! How shameful it is that you don't go and see the wonders in the forest!'

The king was so angry at being called a coward that he shook with rage and awoke. But then he reconsidered: perhaps he was a cowardly king indeed! He summoned a squire to harness his horse – and quietly, so that the queen wouldn't know – and then donned an unmarked surcoat and hid his shield in a cloth cover, and set off into the forest without anyone knowing he'd gone.

It was the most beautiful forest he'd ever seen, smooth and clear of undergrowth, with tall and well-spaced trees. Beneath a huge laurel he saw a lovely spring, and went there to drink. Suddenly a statue on a pillar gave a great blast on a horn, and King Betis looked to his right and saw a knight in full armour galloping towards him on a charger, crying:

'Stay where you are, you rogue! You've done wrong!'

'What wrong have I done, sir knight?'

'You've drunk from the spring without leave.'

'Well truly,' the king said, 'that's hardly a serious crime: water should be common property!'

'Mount and come to prison,' the knight replied. 'There you'll see how serious it is!'

'You'd have an easy victory, sir, if I went to prison just because you told me to!'

'By my gods!' cried the knight. 'You'll come whether it's with good grace or bad!'

And Betis said: 'It'll have to be bad: the only way I'm going is by force.'

'Mount then,' said the knight, 'and defend yourself. Tonight you'll be lying in the wrong kind of bed!'

'Right!' said the king. 'We'll see who'll come off worse!'

And he leapt straight from the ground into his saddle, checked his arms were in order and thrust in his spurs.

They clashed, and both delivered fearsome blows with their lances; but while the knight's missed its target, the king's pierced his enemy's mailcoat and cut through to the bone. The knight took to flight and the king spurred after him, chasing as fast as he could. Then the knight cast a spell: a rushing river a hundred feet wide appeared between him and the king. But the king, his attention fixed on pursuing the knight, intent on not losing his trail, never once looked down and didn't see the river; he carried on the chase without fear. But his horse saw it and was about to rear, and the king, heedless of the danger, still intent on the knight, thrust in his spurs with all his might. His horse leapt from all four hooves fully fifteen feet as if to dive into the river; but when it landed on solid earth instead of the expected water it stumbled and staggered and crashed to the ground, and the king now looked down and thought he was in a river and was dumbfounded; he beat at his horse as though to make him swim, and the bewildered horse clambered up and thrashed around as if swimming, and found himself free of the enchantment and back on level ground. The king now looked ahead and saw the knight a long way off, and began to yell after him:

'It's no use, I tell you! You won't escape!'

The knight heard this and cast another spell: the king thought two lions were charging and attacking him from both sides. He drew his sword and struck one of the lions with all his strength, desperate to be off after the knight, but the blow slashed down without touching anything and plunged a full foot into the ground. Feeling no contact when he should have sliced the lion in half, the king was bewildered;

but he struck again, only for the blow to fall the same way. At this the king realised it was a spell, and said he would leave this buffoonery and tarry no longer; he thrust in his spurs again and his horse, in terror of the lions, charged away with astonishing speed. The lions pursued briefly, but then the spell was over. King Betis looked ahead and saw the knight a fair way off, but he'd stopped to see what the king would do. Betis called after him:

'You're going to die, by God, despite your enchantments!'

And he spurred after him; and the knight cast a spell to make the king think he was turning back to joust. When the king saw the phantom coming towards him he was sure it was the knight with levelled lance, and he set his own lance in its rest and fixed himself in the stirrups and prepared to meet the knight with a deadly thrust. His horse likewise, well trained in combat, braced itself to take the force of collision; and when the exchange of blows came the king was convinced he'd struck the knight clean through the body: he'd put all his force into the thrust; but his horse, preparing to take the impact, met with thin air and buckled at the knees while the king followed through and pitched forward and fell. But chance was with him and he was quite unhurt, and leapt up swiftly and realised it was a spell. He jumped straight back in the saddle and cried:

'I swear, false knight, you'll not escape me!'

And he galloped after him, but had ridden a full league before he caught up.

Outside a castle beside a river, watched by a young lady from a turret above the gate, they joined in battle a second time. They broke their lances and brought each other to the ground, so they drew their swords and clashed in fearsome combat; the knight smashed a hundred rings from the king's mailcoat, but the king dealt an even fiercer blow which fell on the left shoulder and slashed through the chainmail and into the flesh and right down the bone, nerves and sinews as far as the elbow. The knight struck back with a blow that smashed through the king's shield and into his shoulder and through the mail and into the flesh. The bright red blood surged and flowed down to his spurs, and the king was incensed to feel himself wounded and launched himself at the knight and began to batter him with all his might. The combat raged exhaustingly, but it was the knight who tired the more and began to give ground, until he said to the king:

'I pray you, sir knight, stop a while and let me talk to you.'

'Very gladly,' said the king.

And he drew back, and the knight said: 'I've been lord of this forest for forty years: I won it in my youth by force of arms from the most valiant man alive in his time, and ever since then I've triumphed over anyone who tried to put me down. Then just the other day I cast a spell to see how long I would live, and was told it would be until a king reigns in Britain named Perceforest. So tell me your true name, I pray you, and if you're king of England.'

The king was amazed by the knight's words and told him: 'Truly, sir, I know nothing about your death, but I'm king of England by the hand of King Alexander. But my name's not Perceforest: since you ask, my name is Betis de Feson, and my father was Gadifer du Lairis.'

Hearing this, the knight didn't think Betis would be the cause of his death. But he would, for the name Perceforest had been waiting for Betis for twenty years. The knight said: 'Let me go from this battle, and I'll let you return to your country.'

'I promise you, sir,' the king replied, 'once you've escaped me I'll return to my country without your help! Tell me your name and then I'll say what I'll do for you.'

'Since you wish to know, sir, I'll tell you. My name is Darnant the Enchanter, and the forest is named the Darnant Forest after me. Now let me go.'

'Truly,' said the king, 'you'll leave without your head unless you admit defeat and promise to do as I ask.'

'Never!' said the knight.

When the king heard this he raised his sword and dealt him such a blow that he laid him out on the ground with a grievous wound to the head. Then he pulled off the knight's helm, and Darnant cried:

'Ah, noble sir, don't kill me! I'll do as you ask!'

So the king drew back his hand and said: 'Swear it first!'

And as he said this, he saw before him the dwarf who'd appeared in his dream, who said to him: 'Ah, noble king, cut off his head and set free the forest and the land! And do it for your own sake, too, for you'll be dishonoured if he escapes!'

Then the king heard the young lady, watching the battle from the turret above the castle gate, cry: 'Oh, noble king, cut off his head!'

And hearing this, the king said to Darnant: 'You must die.'

And he raised his sword to cut off his head, and took hold of his hair and was about to strike; but it seemed to him that he was holding the hair of the most beautiful maiden he'd ever beheld; and he looked into her face and saw that it was the fair Ydorus, his wife, the queen! He was dumbfounded and said: 'Oh, my love, is it you?'

And it seemed to him that she replied: 'Yes indeed, my love! Have mercy on me!'

The dwarf kept yelling like crazy: 'Noble king, kill him or you're dead!'

But his appeals were vain: the king was sitting beside Darnant embracing him as if he were his wife and saying: 'My sweet love, forgive me for wronging you: I've been deceived!'

And at that Darnant drew a Welsh dagger and stabbed the king in the chest with such force that it went clean through him, but with the help of God it was in his right side just below the shoulder. The king leapt up in shock at the blow and the dwarf cried again:

'Kill him, king, or you're dead!'

Feeling the cruel wound the king realised he'd been bewitched, and he raised his sword and cut off the knight's head. The body stretched out and the soul departed to its due destination. Evil spirits filled the forest with an appalling din, while the dwarf rode off with Darnant's head to announce his death. Then a beautiful young lady arrived and tended to Betis's wound – 'gladly,' she said, 'for he's delivered me and the whole land from that demon!' – and led him back to the castle where all the people, knowing he'd killed their lord, cried:

'Welcome to King Perceforest, who has pierced and purged[2] the evil ways of this forest!'

So they said as they celebrated the death of their lord. Then the lady led him to the main tower where she treated him with all joy and honour, summoning all the ladies and maidens of the castle to cheer and comfort the king. And she said to them:

'Ladies and damsels, greet this knight with joy, for know that this is King Perceforest, whose coming has long been prophesied by Darnant.'

---

[2] 'perchié et ouvert'. There is a play on words here concerning the name Perceforest. The idea is quite complex: he has 'pierced' the forest in terms both of 'penetrating' it as others feared to do and of 'lancing' it to purge infection.

When the king heard this he said: 'Tell me in all honesty, lady: why do you call me Perceforest?'

'Darnant,' she replied, 'the knight you've killed, was one of the most accomplished men in the forests of England in sorcery, spells and enchantments, and he inflicted the most harm with them. He would take by force or love or magic any beautiful lady or maiden within his reach; in consequence there are at least sixty bastards living in this forest, all of them knights, and every one of them engages in magic. Indeed there are fully fifty more due to be knighted in the spring! Less than a week ago he wanted to see how many children his sons had, but he couldn't count them all! It was foretold to him that he'd be killed by a king of England named Perceforest, but he used to tell us that he'd live as long as he liked, because he had spies in England to learn of any man there called Perceforest, and he said that as soon as he heard tell of one he'd have him killed. But the prediction has deceived him! When he heard that Alexander was about to create a new king in England he was very alarmed and sent men to discover his name, but it was reported that the king was called Betis, so he told us he had nothing to fear from him. How wrong he was! For now, sir, we know that the name Perceforest is yours, and you are welcome indeed!'

The Perilous Temple

Perceforest is set in the pre-Christian past. The pagan Alexander is a paragon of every chivalrous quality, and the 'old gods' he worships are undoubtedly abroad and functioning in the world; but there is a fascinating tension throughout the romance between this old religion and the 'New Law' of Christianity which is to be brought to Britain at the story's end. Perceforest is shortly to learn of a new 'Sovereign God' at a mysterious round temple, but in this earlier passage Alexander encounters the temple's terrors before him.

Alexander and Floridas rode all day until they met a cowherd at the foot of a steep mountain. He told them it was the Mount of the Marvel, where none but knights ever ventured. Intrigued, they climbed to the top and found it planted thick with oaks, and the grass came up to their horses' knees. They rode along the mountain top and came across a great expanse of holly trees so dense that they couldn't see a foot inside. The king said to Floridas:

'Here's a sturdy hedge indeed!'

They rode along the outside till they found a narrow gap where horses had passed quite recently, but they had to dismount and pull their horses by the reins and walk some distance through the dense holly-wood, and they reached the other side covered in scratches. But they emerged to find themselves in a beautiful spot, in the middle of which stood a round temple.

On its eastern side was a porch suggesting an entrance, and seeing this, the king said to Floridas: 'Let's go and worship in the temple.'

Alexander went ahead and strode straight to the temple door; but as he was about to enter and set his front foot on the threshold, he couldn't help bowing his head, because the light had a special, pure quality, its only source being precious stones: there were four carbuncles – four bright red gems – ingeniously placed in the temple; they shone their light at a mirror, and its reflection cast such a radiance in the temple that every corner was clearly visible; it wasn't as bright as day, but the whole place was beautified by the quality of the light. But then, as Alexander looked down at the floor, it seemed to him that it was nothing but an abyss, and an abyss moreover planted with bristling spears, points upward, so many that they were only a foot apart! The king was aghast and drew back in horror, realising he'd have faced certain death if he'd taken another step forward. Floridas was amazed to see him so afraid and said:

'What's the matter, my lord?'

'Go and look through the temple door and you'll know – but don't go in!'

Floridas went straight to the door and looked down at the floor and saw the terrifying sight. He said to himself it was a place designed for murder! Then he turned his gaze towards the ceiling and saw that just as the floor was bristling with spears, so was the ceiling hung with them, and every one seemed on the point of falling. He was horrified and turned back and said to the king:

'My lord, come and see this: it's amazing!'

He pointed to the ceiling, and Alexander said it was the most perilous place he'd ever seen and must have been made to trap intruders.

'But it's not unfrequented, I'd say.' He could see a beautiful altar at the far end of the temple, enclosed by curtains. 'I think there are priests here: I can see an altar, but I don't know which gods are worshipped.'

'You're right,' said Floridas. 'But I can't imagine where they stand: I can see no way in or out of the temple but here, and no one who cares for his life can enter this way unless he flies through the air by magic!'

The king replied that he could see a little door near the altar. 'Let's see if anyone opens it: then we can talk to him.'

So they sat down on the threshold and waited for a good hour, but no one came in at all.

Then they heard two horses whinny outside and knew they weren't their own; Floridas guessed there must be some kind of dwelling nearby, so they went out and walked half way round the temple and saw a handsome house close by. Eager to find someone who could explain what they'd seen, they came to the door of a hall, huge and beautiful and perfectly round, with a pillar in the middle supporting the vaulted ceiling of the hall, which was built entirely of stone. As soon as they reached the door and looked inside, they saw two knights, fully armed, gazing at the pillar. They were Gadifer and Le Tor, and the four knights greeted each other with delight.

All four had seen the perilous entrance to the temple, and Gadifer now showed them another wonder: hung upon the pillar of the hall was a gold shield blazoned with a blue lamp burning a red flame, and an inscription declared that it would belong to any knight who could take it down. Gadifer and Le Tor had already tried and failed, and now Alexander's face turned red with fruitless effort and Floridas tried and might as easily have moved the temple as unhooked that shield. They were amazed and said that evidently the one had not yet come who was to take down the shield: it must have been hung there for some mysterious reason and there was none among them worthy to unhook it. Whereupon they heard a man's voice say:

'Indeed, sirs, you're right! Be gone!'

And they heard a window of the hall slam shut. Alexander appealed to a man on the other side of the window to open it and speak to him, and hearing that 'your tongue sounds Greek' the man did so, saying: 'If you'd been one of the knights of the forest this window would never have opened, but it will for you.'

He was an elderly man; Alexander asked him if he was the master of the house, but he proved to be only a servant, and he told the king that no one who'd come to the place had ever spoken to its lord. Alexander accepted that, but told the old man that the place alarmed him: 'It seems you're out to murder honest folk as soon as they set foot in the temple!'

The old man told him he was quite mistaken, saying: 'If your sight hadn't been darkened by the shadows of sin, you wouldn't have been so misguided in what you saw. The place isn't made to deceive people but to receive the worthy, for it's a holy place. You surely know that opposites cannot attract or join; they always repel and stay apart. So it is with you: the place is such that the worthy and the holy can enter and encounter nothing to alarm or oppose them but are naturally welcome there, while you, stained with misbelief and other sins, as soon as you came near the holy place were filled with fear and terror of your opposite; for it seemed to you that all the good things residing in the temple were threatening weapons. Good being opposite to evil, the good will always see the evil as knives and swords, and the bad will see the good as swords and spears. So don't speak ill of the temple or its guardian, for the place was created in the cause of good and its guardian intends nothing else.'

Alexander was dumbfounded by the old man's words, but he spoke up and said to him: 'Sir, you say I've been rejected from the place because of my sins and my wrongful belief. In all my ventures the gods have never suggested I'm out of favour with them! The gods of the sea, the earth and the sky have backed me in all I've done, for which I give them thanks and praise.'

'Ah, sir knight,' said the old man, 'the more they've elevated you, the more reason you have to fear, for the gods in whom you believe can do nothing but bad! And however much people may think they've gained from them, their belief is wildly mistaken. Fortune, playing with worldly wealth and honour and randomly giving more to one than another, just as mindlessly takes it away when she pleases. It reminds me that the lord of this place told me not a month ago that this year would see one of the greatest wonders that has ever occurred since the world began: eleven years ago there appeared a bird in Greece that has since grown to an unimaginable size, and by the last day of this year it will have grown so great that it will have outgrown the world, spreading its wings over all the earth, but the next day I could cover that bird with my mantle! I said to my lord: "Truly, sir, that's a wonder indeed, but tell me your meaning more clearly." And he replied: "Ask no more." But it seems to me that Fortune and the evil spirits who hide in the idols of misbelievers do nothing but mock and deceive the men made rich and mighty by Fortune.'

Alexander was shaken by this and said: 'Good sir, could you please arrange for us to speak to this lord of yours?'

'Truly, sir knight, no one will speak to him until he's spoken to the one who's destined to take down that shield.'

The destined one is Perceforest himself, who in the following passage encounters the temple just as Alexander had done, and learns about the 'Sovereign God'.

Just like Alexander and Floridas before him, when Perceforest came to the threshold he saw a brilliant light inside and an altar veiled by curtains, and, to his alarm, the floor twenty cubits below and bristling thick with spears – as was the ceiling. He sat and kept watch till midnight.

Then he saw an old man, with amazingly long white hair and a thick white beard, draw back the curtains that hid the altar, whereupon he could clearly see that on it was a richly crafted cabinet, all of fine gold; and inside it, hung on golden chains, was a beautiful lamp, brightly burning with oil as clear as crystal. Its flame was extraordinary: as it rose, the single flame divided into three in wondrous fashion: the one in the centre was white as snow and soared higher than the two beside it, the one at its right hand was red as blood, and the one at its left was the colour of natural fire.[3] The king gazed in wonder at the lamp and its flame, and longed to know what it signified. He looked too at the worthy man who took a censer of fine gold and made three turns of the altar, purifying the surrounding air with incense. Then he stood before it and bowed deeply before walking away across the spears as though on thin air.

Suddenly the man had disappeared, and Perceforest was furious with himself for having asked him nothing. He waited for him to return – but he didn't, much to his frustration. Then he picked up his lance to lean on while he took a short nap – he didn't want to lie down in case he slept too long. And as he turned his lance on end he felt it touch the temple floor, which he'd taken to be twenty cubits below. He couldn't understand what it had hit, and he took his lance and tapped where it had struck, and felt it make contact with something – but he couldn't tell what. It seemed there was indeed a floor less than half a foot below the threshold. He swept his lance from side to side and felt it move across something as smooth as ice and solid as stone. He felt sure there was magic at work, and stretched out his foot from the threshold to see if it was true; and just inches inside the temple it met the floor, firm and hard as stone. He started stamping, but the floor was strong and sure. He resolved to walk across – he would die but once! – and as soon as he stood up he found the floor was perfectly solid. So he took his helm and set it on his head, slung his shield around his neck and took his lance in hand, ready to defend himself if the need arose. Then he began to walk across the floor; but however solid it felt, his blood pumped and his heart pounded as he looked at the spears below, for he saw no more floor beneath his feet than if he'd been walking on thin air. On he stepped in fear and dread until

---

[3]   'feu materiel': this seems to be an allusion to the Pentecostal tongues of fire (Acts 2, 1-4) and therefore symbolic of the Holy Spirit. The tripartite flame surely symbolises the Trinity, with the white and tallest representing God the Father and the red at its right hand God the Son.

he reached the altar, where he found the floor spread with bearskins: he felt a little more secure with these beneath him, the spears being out of sight. He looked all about: he could see as clearly as if a dozen torches had been burning, yet there was no candle or fire to be seen. Then he decided to worship, to pray to the gods for mercy, for he felt sure it was a sacred place. So he withdrew to a corner behind the altar and started praying to his god Mars and to his goddess Venus and to several others to whom he always prayed. But as soon as he uttered their names everything went black about him, as if his eyes had been gouged out, and something, he didn't know what, struck him such a blow on the helm that he lost consciousness for some while.

When he came to his senses he realised a spear had crashed down on to his chainmailed back; it hadn't pierced his flesh but had gone through the mail and plunged so deep into the floor that he couldn't pull it out; nor could he stand: his hauberk was pinned there. He was very frightened then, and began to pray to Neptune and Diana and the gods of the sea for help, and as soon as he uttered this prayer two spears came plummeting down on him. One flashed so close to the flesh of his chest that it grazed his breast, pierced his thigh armour and stuck so deep in the floor that he couldn't pull it free; the second smashed right through his shield, the point plunging between his legs at the groin and ramming into the floor so hard that the shield was forced down on him, crushing him like a millstone. Feeling so trapped, so pinned that he could neither move nor summon enough voice to be heard, he truly feared he was about to die: he couldn't move a muscle or his tongue to summon help; and he thought he'd no longer appeal to the gods for mercy as they were clearly against him – he'd wait for someone to take pity, though he didn't know who.

As he lay there expecting nothing but death, Perceforest heard loud footsteps crossing the floor, then the curtains being opened at the altar, and then someone devoutly offering a metrical, rhymed prayer:

> 'Almighty God of unknown form
> Who have created all things known,
> Grant us the mind to recognise you.
> In this barrenness, belief in you
> Has turned to deepening ignorance.

The people cling to a misplaced faith,
Believing wrongly in many gods.
Now, God, show them the error of their ways -
Do not delay!
Philosophy has proved since its infancy
That there is but one God, with power over all.
He is the true God and in him lies true happiness;
He is the hook on which the whole world hangs
        and depends.
Wise philosophers have placed their faith in him
And worship him; they believe in no other.

God omnipotent, show us you are lord!
As yet your triple body
Has not taken mortal form.
If you wish to bestow your grace upon mankind
And let them truly conceive of you,
Dress yourself in our body.
As yet your beauty is hidden from us
But we long for you, so show yourself
And find a way to heal us and return us to the path
        of truth
By making a mortal body from your divine body,
For we are dying through our sin
In obeying numerous gods.

Mankind, do not be so misguided
As to worship any longer
Golden idols or painted panels.
Mars and Jupiter have no power or substance,
And Venus counts for nothing save through Love,
        her son.
So cast them all out, believe in them no longer
And let us turn to God,
Who sees us all through a narrow window
Where he sits on his mighty throne
In his glory, the source of all true treasure,
Which is where our home should be.'

When Perceforest heard the worthy man's voice and his prayer, uttered with such passion that the sighs from the depths of his heart brought tears streaming from Perceforest's eyes and down his cheeks, he said to himself that he knew exactly why this misadventure had befallen him, and it was well deserved: indeed, almighty God had shown him great mercy in treating him no more harshly! And he vowed in his heart – being incapable of speech – that he would never again worship numerous gods, for he was sure this was why he'd been brought to such a pass. He began earnestly to repent of having done so before, and said he was glad indeed to have abandoned his foolish belief thanks to hearing the worthy man's prayer. Then he made his own devout prayer, saying:

'Ah, God unequalled, God above all things, have mercy on me!'

And as soon as he uttered these words he felt his trouble lighten, and sensed he could have spoken had there been someone to hear – though he was still unable to move, being pinned there by the spears. Then he heard the worthy man who'd said the prayer closing the curtain around the altar, and he called out: 'Ah, worthy sir, in the name of the Sovereign God, have pity on a poor sinner who needs your help!"

The worthy man called him forward, but Perceforest said he could move nothing but his tongue! So the man came to him and saw him pinned to the floor, and guessed it was because of his foolish beliefs.

'Dear friend,' he said, 'tell me how you come to be here.'

And Perceforest told the worthy man all that had befallen him.

'Well,' he replied, 'if you're truly resolved to believe in God omnipotent who created all the world, and to reject all others, I'm sure you'll be set free, but not otherwise.'

'Truly, sir,' said Perceforest, 'I believe in him and am certain none of the other gods has the power to harm or help me.'

When the worthy man heard the knight say he would renounce all the gods and live firmly in belief in the Sovereign God, he came to him and started pulling out the spears until he'd completely freed him. Then he bade him rise, which he did at once, as happy as he had ever been in his life. Then he stepped up to the altar and prayed to the god of Nature to forgive him for having so long failed to acknowledge him, and promised to believe in him all the days of his life.

The Adventures of Claudius and Estonné

Perceforest has many deep and intriguing themes. It is also – perhaps even first and foremost – a rich and thrilling entertainment, featuring numerous sequences of which the director of a modern 'action movie' would be proud. The adventures of two knights as they search for the missing King Perceforest offer some particularly memorable examples.

After dividing from Alexander and the others in the search for Perceforest, the English knight Claudius and the Scottish lord Estonné[4] rode for three days without incident – or indeed food. They were hungry – unsurprisingly, though the people in those days were of a stronger constitution and were not so richly fed. But Estonné caught sight of a herd of deer and, being an excellent hunter, quickly made a kill. Then he cut off a leg and said:

'Now, my noble companion, you shall eat – and so shall I!'

'We would indeed, if we had a fire,' said Claudius.

'By my father's soul,' said Estonné, 'I'll prepare and cook it in the manner of my country, well suited to a wandering knight.'

And he drew his sword and stepped up to a tree; he made a deep cut in a branch and split it open for a good two feet and rammed in the leg. Then he took the halter from his horse and bound it round the branch and pulled so tight that the blood and fluids were squeezed from the flesh to leave it sweet and dry, and finished by skinning it to leave the meat as white as a capon's.

'There, sir!' he said to Claudius. 'That's how we cook it in my country! Eat as heartily as you like – I'll take the first bite.'

And he reached into a pouch he kept by his saddle and produced salt and a powdered blend of pepper and ginger which he threw on and rubbed in good and hard. He cut the meat in half and gave one piece to Claudius, and then bit into the other so hungrily that he sent the powder flying. Seeing him eat with such gusto made Claudius feel ravenous and he tucked in with a will. Then he said to Estonné:

[4]   The name implies 'giddy', 'scatter-brained'.

'Upon my soul, I've never eaten meat prepared like this! But from now on I wouldn't go out of my way to have the cooked variety!'

'When I'm in the wilds of Scotland,' said Estonné, 'I'll ride a week or a fortnight without finding a castle or a house or seeing a fire or any living soul except wild beasts – and this is the way I eat them! And I wouldn't swap it for the meat of the emperor!'

After eating they rode down to a spring.

'Let's quench our thirst,' said Estonné, 'with the drink the great God has provided for all men: I prefer it to the beers of England!'

But while they were drinking, two knights suddenly rode down, killed their horses as they grazed, and galloped back into the forest. Estonné and Claudius, shocked and enraged, recovered their saddles and set off into the woods to find out why the knights had done this. Moments later they saw seven knights ride down to the spring and heard them say: 'They've fled. We've lost them.'

'Claudius dear friend,' whispered Estonné, 'keep quiet and let me handle things with my lance: we'll kill all seven. They've slaughtered our horses so that they can kill us more easily, but we'll have theirs if it please the great God.'

The seven now turned and rode towards the spinney where Estonné and Claudius had taken cover. At their head was Dragon, one of Darnant's sons, and he was saying: 'I'm sorry we killed their horses now: it's made them run into the forest in fear.'

When Estonné heard this he leapt from the trees, lance in his right hand and shield at his left, and cried: 'We're not here to hide but to find you! You killed our horses without a challenge and we'll kill you likewise! Get ready – you're about to feel my lance!'

And he launched it with such mighty force that it went clean through Dragon, carried on through the man behind him and didn't stop until it hit the shield of a third. Dragon and the second knight toppled dead, and the other five were horrified. But they charged at Estonné, and Claudius leapt from his hiding-place in support. A furious combat followed in which four of the knights were killed and the fifth took to flight. Claudius grabbed a horse and galloped after him, but Estonné couldn't find a mount: all the other horses had bolted into the forest. He howled with frustration, but seeing that yelling would do no good he started to race like a madman across the open fields to see if he could find a horse. He saw a herd of mares in a valley; there was a young one in the middle, particularly big and strong, and he decided to catch her, even though at that time there was no greater disgrace for a knight than to ride a mare and no knight mindful of his own honour would joust with one so mounted. But Estonné, with no thought for his own shame, only for his friend's need of help, plunged into the middle of the herd and caught the mare. He recovered the harness and saddle of his dead horse to use on her, and finding that every lance on the battleground was broken, he rescued a lance-head and, resourceful as ever, used his sword to cut a branch of yew to make a mightily strong – if crude – new shaft. Then he set off after Claudius.

Claudius meanwhile had chased the knight for three leagues till they came to a fast-flowing river. The knight knew he had no choice but to jump in or die, so he sent his horse diving straight in, and Claudius, thinking it would be shameful to give up the chase, plunged in after him, sword drawn, and caught up with him right in mid-current. Then he raised his sword and struck the knight such a blow on the helm that he lost his stirrups and keeled over; and when his head was under water he grabbed hold of the skirt of Claudius's mailcoat with an unbreakable grip. He was drowned in seconds nonetheless, but as the two horses swam on, one forward, one backward, the dead knight clung so tightly to Claudius that he couldn't tear him off and the horses couldn't take the weight and began to drown. Seeing this, Claudius struck the knight's arm with his sword and cut it clean off, leaving the hand still hanging from his hauberk. Now free of the body he thrust in his spurs but his horse couldn't move: it was drowning beneath him. A moment later he felt his horse was no longer carrying him; he was up to his neck in the water and feared he was about to die: he was drinking rather more than he needed! He started thrashing around with his arms and legs to save himself if he could, but his armour was weighing him down and the water overwhelmed him: he swallowed so much that he lost strength and consciousness, and in this desperate state he was swept a league downstream.

The torrent carried him straight into the net of two fishermen: they'd cast it into the river to catch fish to take to the gathering of the knights at the city of Darnantes. As they hauled their net from the water they found a man inside.

'Ah!' cried one of the fishermen. 'We've caught a corpse!'

Meanwhile at a great gathering of Darnant's clan in the city of Darnantes, the dead enchanter's sons had made new knights of fully a
hundred of their kinsmen, and one of them, Aigret, mustered a company of thirty to go hunting for the supporters of Perceforest. They
rode deep into the forest; and while they were arranging themselves
into several bands they looked through the trees and saw an armed
knight approaching. He was riding like a wild thing, without direction or control; and as he drew near they saw he was mounted on a
mare, causing one of them to say to his fellows:

'Here comes a disgraced knight – he's of no value – from him
you'll win only shame and reproach!'

When the knight caught sight of them he called out a challenge, but
they ignored him because of the mare; he was furious, and gripped
his lance, which he'd hewn from a tree-branch, so sturdy and strong
that it was unbreakable, and charged. He ploughed straight through
one band, right through a second, on through a third, a fourth, a fifth,
a sixth, and then galloped away without stopping, leaving six knights
dead in his wake. When Aigret's companions saw what had hit them,
so shockingly and suddenly, and realised that six of their fellows had
been killed by a disgraced knight riding a mare, they were so aghast
and confused that they couldn't take it in and thought it must have
been a dream. Aigret roused them, saying:

'We must hunt him down and kill him before he can boast of this!
We've been more shamed here than if we'd all been mounted on
mares in the middle of the city of Darnantes!'

They set off in pursuit, and as evening fell they caught sight of him
still riding like a madman, giving no impression of knowing where
he was going. They hurried after him but had trouble catching up
with his impressively fit and spirited mare. Aigret finally drew near,
and the knight, sensing him close behind, switched his lance from
right hand to left and drew his sword without drawing rein. Aigret
cried out to him:

'Shamed knight, turn and lessen your disgrace!'

When the knight heard this, he reined in his mare and, without
turning to look, struck Aigret a backhand blow that sent his severed
head flying into the middle of the field. Then he spurred his mare
forward and went on his way. When the knights behind saw this they
were horrified, and realised he was shaming them more and more,

but they continued the chase, for the valiant among them preferred to die in honour than live in such disgrace. And truly, every time the knight sensed them close behind, he would suddenly stop when they were least expecting it and slice off their heads with a backhand sweep. He killed fully twelve like this, and when the others saw they couldn't catch him and that he'd now killed eighteen of their companions in this mad pursuit, they drew rein, confounded, and let him go.

The Wonders at Gadifer's Coronation

If the martial exploits of Claudius and Estonné are fanciful and wishful thinking, reflecting the period's fantasies like many a modern gunfight or car chase, so are some of the passages in Perceforest describing the glamour attendant upon kingship. Enchantment is again a notable feature as the author tells of the coronation of Perceforest's brother Gadifer as king of Scotland.

That morning King Gadifer and Queen Lydore left the temple of Mars and made their way in a magnificent procession to the place of coronation, where a great scaffold had been built so that the vast crowd who'd gathered there would be able to see clearly. And as they approached the scaffold they saw that a vine had grown above it, casting enough shadow all around to shade two thousand people, and so laden with grapes that there were as many bunches as leaves. The common folk wondered what this fruit could be, for there had never been a vine in the country before; and the nobility, who did recognise it, wondered even more how the vine could be so leafy and in fruit – not due before September – when it was the first day of April.

'Truly,' said Alexander, 'the gods are performing miracles at our king's coronation: it's a sign of blessing and prosperity!'

In the shade of the vine all the princes and knights assembled, and Alexander led King Gadifer by the hand to his throne on the scaffold, while the queen was escorted to hers by Perceforest and Porrus. Then Le Tor and Estonné mounted the scaffold bearing the crowns, and Alexander took the king's and raised it high and placed it on Gadifer's head, saying:

'With all honour and reverence to the Superlative God, I confer this royal crown upon you, and may it bring you the wisdom, power and will to govern and maintain this kingdom in every way to its honour and to its people's benefit.'

With similar words he crowned the queen. Then Gadifer rose from his throne and Alexander took his place, and the king of Scotland knelt and paid homage to the noble emperor, accepting the kingdom as his liegeman. So great was the joy that erupted then that you wouldn't have heard God's thunder.

Then they came down from the scaffold and mounted and rode to the tables prepared for the banquet outside the castle: they were set up in a great circle so that everyone could see each other; and a mighty wonder occurred: the vine that had shaded the king and all the knights at the coronation followed them like a cloud, for it was a beautiful day and the sun was as hot as if it had been May.

When everyone was seated it was an astounding sight: there were fully three thousand knights and ladies at that banquet. And as the dishes were served to them, strange wonders occurred: first a squire appeared and produced chaplets of roses for every knight and maiden present, delivering them with such speed that everyone was baffled as to how he could have distributed so many so quickly; and then he vanished – no one knew what had become of him. And when the knights had placed the chaplets on the maidens' heads, they all found that they were suddenly – and all at the same time – holding their partners gently by the chin, their faces so close that a kiss was surely imminent! The spell that had brought this about then broke, but it didn't stop most of the kisses being given and received! Alexander himself went through with it! Finding himself so close to the sweet face of his beloved Sebile, he couldn't resist kissing her – and she permitted it before turning her face away.

Then, just as the servants brought dishes of rabbit and were poised to carve them for their lords, they suddenly saw a boy in hunting garb with a goat's horn in his hand. He put it to his lips and blew the horn, and as soon as it sounded the banqueters saw the rabbits in the platters before them leap up and go running round the tables pursued by hounds as swiftly as in an open field, and the knights and ladies snatched their cups and goblets clear for fear they'd all be spilt. After a few moments the hounds caught all the rabbits, the huntsman sounded the catch, and the knights and ladies looked back at their plates and saw the rabbits all lying there, cooked.

They ate heartily, if mystified, and then were served with a variety of wildfowl. But just as the squires were about to carve, four noble youths appeared in their midst, two holding handsome sparrowhawks and two holding falcons. They removed their jesses and set them free, whereupon the knights and ladies saw the cooked birds spring up and fly for their lives. If you'd been there you'd have seen the sparrowhawks make the most awesome swoops upon the bitterns and the herons. It was a joyous spectacle, as the sparrowhawks dipped and wheeled around the herons to attack them from behind, and the herons snapped back with their beaks to try to save their lives; but they couldn't stop the hawks savaging their bodies and breasts till their hearts broke and they came raining down on the tables, so thick and fast that everyone was amazed that two sparrowhawks could bring down so many birds. But there was more entertainment still: the falcons, who'd circled so high that they were lost to view, saw mallards and other birds fly up from the tables, and came swooping like thunderbolts time and again, sending them plummeting to the ground in such numbers that it was amazing that they could rise and swoop at such speed. In rapt delight the company sat watching the birds tourney in the air until the four youths called their hawks back to their wrists; then suddenly the knights and ladies and maidens had no idea where they'd gone – but there before them were their dishes of wildfowl, cut up and ready to eat.

The last course was pressed spiced fawn, the supreme, most sumptuous dish of the time, and a quarter of a fawn was served in each dish. And when every table had been served the knights and ladies looked up and saw a man dressed in deerskin with a huge club over his shoulder and a long beard and a mane of shaggy hair. Suddenly he started bellowing like a stag, and in an instant the place was full of hinds belling in anguish as if they'd lost their fawns. And it seemed to everyone, knights and ladies alike, that the quartered fawns in their platters leapt to the ground and joined together four by four and suddenly were whole again and bleating tenderly as infants to mothers; and each mother appeared to run to her son and suckle him. The company watched in utter delight; and a moment later the wild man with his club gave a loud whistle, whereupon the hinds set off towards the forest with their fawns bounding joyously after them.

King Gadifer's Wound

More than once the author of Perceforest, emphasising the need he sees for strong, sound rule, tells us that 'when the head is sick, all the limbs suffer'. For a significant period both brothers crowned by Alexander – Perceforest in England and Gadifer in Scotland – are incapacitated and unable to give leadership to their kingdoms. Perceforest is so overcome by grief at the news of Alexander's death that he sinks into a long and debilitating depression, and the following episode tells what happens to Gadifer while hunting.

Six leagues from the castle they passed into a vast forest, and beside a stream from a spring they saw the ground interestingly disturbed. Le Tor was sure they were the marks of 'the hugest, mightiest boar I ever saw: he's caused me more trouble than any other!' King Gadifer was eager to see the beast, so Le Tor sent his escort ahead to find lodging while he and the king rode into the woods with some huntsmen and a pack of hounds.

They'd been searching for some time when suddenly, in a ditch in the shade of a massive oak, they saw the boar lying fast asleep.

'My lord,' said one of the huntsmen, 'I'll go and kill him while he's sleeping: he looks so strong that no dogs of ours could bring him down or wear him out in flight – he'd kill them all in his first attack!'

'What, man?' said the king. 'You may be a beast-murderer but we're not! I want the thrill of the chase, and to kill him with a bow!'

'Do as you please, my lord,' said the huntsman, 'but it's said here in the forest that whoever kills that boar is destined to be left a cripple.'

'Hold your tongue,' said the king. 'I don't believe in their omens and soothsayings.'

The noble king wouldn't heed the huntsman's words – which was a great pity for him and a great woe for the kingdom of Scotland. For had he remained hale in body, all honour, all nobility, all prowess would have come to Scotland and it would have been the home and the fount of all chivalry.

But the noble king, fearing nothing, spurred his mount forward and came up to the boar, asleep in its ditch, and said: 'Up you get, master, you've slept too long! I want to see you on your feet!'

When the boar heard the king it leapt up, startled; and when it saw him it started snorting so loudly that the whole forest rang and those who were nearest were stricken with dread. Then the boar, shaking off its sleep, began to stretch and rear and bristle and pointed its ears straight at the king, so fiercely that any man alive would have felt fear and terror – and with good reason, for it stood chest-high to any knight, and its two tusks sprang a full foot from its maw, whiter than the finest ivory. The king wondered where such a fearsome beast could have come from; but he summoned up his courage and called the hounds to attack. They leapt at the boar from all sides; but the beast was unmoved, and turned its head at a hound that was biting its leg, ripped it open with its tusk and flung the disembowelled dog straight into the king's chest, nearly knocking him from his horse and leaving his breast and face all covered in gore.

Soon every dog was dead, and the boar went charging through the king's astounded company, goring one knight's horse on the way, and plunged into a deep marsh where it set about wallowing in the mud.

King Gadifer now sent Le Tor away to take lodging with the rest of his company, but dispatched huntsmen to the Chastel du Chief to fetch a fresh pack of hounds. As soon as they returned they set off into the marsh where the boar was wallowing in the mire. But the going was so soft that they couldn't get within half a bowshot on horseback, so the huntsmen went ahead on foot and launched the hounds against the boar as it sprawled there in the bog. The dogs knew their business and attacked it from all sides, biting and clawing at its legs and ears. But the boar was proud and wouldn't budge; it lashed out with its tusks as they fastened on its ears; but it had let them get a hold and they stuck to their task and were biting through its hide, tough and age-creased though it was. Realising how hard-pressed it was, the boar bellowed and reared and struck one hound with its tusk, ripping him open right down his spine. Then the other dogs drew back, but the huntsmen drove them to attack again. Watching the vicious fight that followed, Gadifer swore he'd never enjoyed a hunt so much! The boar came running from the marsh and on to firm ground, the dogs still upon it; it turned and attacked and killed four more before tearing away into the forest. The king spurred his horse after it and put his horn to his lips and blew so loud that the whole forest rang. Anthenor and Thelamon followed behind, blowing their horns and hallooing and making such a din, and the huntsmen behind them blasting their horns so loud, that the clamour and the baying could be heard for two long leagues. And the boar, in alarm at the noise, began to snort and bellow so loud that it was dreadful to hear.

As the chase went on every hound was killed or wounded; but the boar had to keep running, for Gadifer, Anthenor and Thelamon were hard on its heels, stabbing its rump with their spears, incensing it till it was foaming with rage and malice. Suddenly it turned on them, and lashing out with its tusk it tore the belly of Anthenor's horse wide open, the bowels spilling on the forest floor. Then it charged away through the forest again, and the king and Thelamon spurred after it, telling Anthenor to wait for the huntsmen and take one of their horses and follow their tracks.

The king and Thelamon chased the boar until they reached a river that flowed through the forest, where they started stabbing at its rump with their spears; the boar turned again and gored Thelamon in the thigh, inflicting a deep wound, and ripped his mount's belly right open so that Thelamon and his horse came crashing down in a heap. Then the boar turned and plunged in the river. The king was speechless with fury; into the water he launched his horse after the beast, which was soon over the river and back on firm ground and charging on into the forest. The king crossed the river as fast as he could and set off in pursuit, overwhelmed with rage that it had wounded Thelamon.

On he rode till night fell, so dark that he could see little or nothing ahead. Then the boar found itself in a marsh again, and when it felt the wetness of the ground it made its way into a muddy runnel to cool down.

The king now decided to withdraw to a nearby thicket and rest his horse and wait for his huntsmen to catch up. He took off his horse's harness and left him to graze, and sat down on a knoll to rest.

But about midnight the boar came out of the marsh, desperately hungry, and headed towards an oak to gather acorns. Seeing this, the king was afraid he might lose him, but he didn't know what to do, for his horse was now unharnessed and grazing away behind him. So he went striding ahead on foot, his sword drawn, crying:

'Hey! Son of a sow! You may have given me and my men some trouble, but you're not going to get away!'

And he raised his sword to strike; but the boar wouldn't give ground and came charging at him in a rage. The king brought his sword down on its forehead, dealing such a blow that the blade plunged four inches into its skull; but the bone was harder than the ivory tusk, and a full foot of the blade broke off and was left sticking from the forehead like a horn; and the boar in its fury tossed its head and struck the noble king a piteous blow with its tusk right at the top of the thigh, severing the nerve where it joined the bone to the hip. Then it charged on by and plunged into the wood. The noble king fell wounded in the thigh, which was a grievous pity for the kingdom of Scotland, for it thereby lost its honour.

Gadifer was losing copious blood and was sure he was going to die, and cried: 'Ah, wicked, treacherous Fortune, how you've deceived me with your smiling face! I thought my strength and power were such that I could challenge the mightiest in the world; now you've turned your back on me and suddenly, without warning, made me feel your cruelty. Ah, Gadifer! Yesterday morning you'd have fought and upheld your rights against the mightiest knight in the world, and now you lie maimed and beaten by a dumb beast armed only with a tooth!'

Soon Gadifer had lost so much blood that he was too weak to utter a word or move a limb. The only sense left to him was sight. But as he gazed ahead, expecting nothing but death, he saw two blazing torches appear, and behind them two maidens dressed in garments whiter than snow; and one of them, who appeared to be in command, said: 'Sir knight, may our god bring you comfort.'

The king was in no state to reply, so the maidens had him carried to a house of theirs, not far from that very spot.

Zephir the Trickster

A key figure in Perceforest, and a most surprising one, is a creature called Zephir. He's a fallen angel, cast out of Paradise along with Lucifer, yet he looks after the interests of several admirable knights and indeed of Britain as a whole. And he's a Puck-like trickster (and, like Puck, unable to tolerate daylight), delighting in playing the most cruel (if often hilarious) tricks on people — and all his powers, he says, 'come from God'. He first appears to Estonné in the 'Selve Carbonneuse' — the area of the Low Countries later known as Brabant and Hainault — where Estonné, assisting Count Le Tor in a campaign on Alexander's behalf, is trying to find a way to take a castle that's resisting a lengthy siege.

Estonné and Narcis rode on until, a little after sundown, they came within a league of Branius's castle. They began to climb a mountain towards a great forest, and it grew so dark that only a glimmer of moonlight lit their way. And then, as they rode, they were astonished to see their helmets and the ears of their horses covered in will o' the wisps — a countless number, flickering all around them so that their path was all aglow. Estonné was amazed. The will o' the wisps kept following them, jostling and swarming like a cloud of gnats, and Estonné said:

'What are these things that are plaguing us?'

'Sir,' Narcis replied, 'in this land they're called will o' the wisps, because they look like wisps of flame; they're often seen in these parts.'

Estonné took hold of a leafy oak-branch and started swishing the air in front of him to beat them away; but it was in vain: far from lessening their number, his branch became covered with the things until it seemed to be on fire! He kept up his fight till he began to ride downhill; as they reached the valley the will o' the wisps were snuffed out by the mist and dampness of the marshes. But now they could see less well than before; and suddenly Estonné, riding ahead, heard a voice say: 'You'll never take the castle without me.'

The voice repeated these words six times in fifty yards, and Estonné said to Narcis: 'Whats that voice that keeps saying 'You'll never take the castle without me?''

'Truly,' Narcis replied, 'I think it must be an imp.'[5]

'An imp? What's that?'

'An invisible spirit,' said Narcis, 'that delights in trickery.'

And Estonné heard the voice, a little further off than before, say: 'I tell you, Estonné, you'll never take it without me.'

'Narcis,' he said, 'wait here till I come back, for death itself won't stop me finding out what this voice means.'

'Oh, no, sir, by almighty God!' said Narcis. 'It's sure to end in grief!'

'I don't know what the end will be, but I'm not stopping till I've found out what it means. Just wait here beneath this tree; I shan't be long.'

And he spurred his horse in the direction of the voice. He hadn't gone far before he heard it say: 'If you want to take the castle, ride to the elm tree up ahead and mount the horse you'll find there, and I'll make sure you get it.'

Estonné looked ahead and saw the elm, and standing beside it the strongest, finest horse he'd ever seen, saddled and harnessed as if for Alexander himself. He thought his luck was in: it was worth four times his own! So he dismounted and tethered his horse to the tree and mounted the one before him; and feeling its sturdiness and power he fixed himself in the stirrups, clutched his lance in his right hand, set his shield at his left, and cried:

'Where are you, who promised me the castle? I'm mounted!'

Not a soul breathed a word in reply. But the horse he'd mounted took the bit between its teeth and charged off through the forest as if possessed by all the devils in Hell, stopping for neither hedge nor thicket but plunging clean through like a mad thing. Estonné's tunic was soon so ripped that every thorn he'd passed had had a share, and before long he'd not enough left to bind a finger. The horse went storming on, unstoppable: to Estonné it seemed to get ever faster, careering through hedge and bush. Mountain or level ground, it made no difference! It headed straight for a thorny thicket, where Estonné lost his lance in the brambles, and his shield, which had been slung

---

[5]   'luiton'. This is a difficult word to translate. It's a shame that 'imp' suggests smallness, but so does 'sprite'; and 'daemon/demon' is too predominantly black and 'goblin' too malicious for the intriguingly ambiguous, shape-changing creature we are about to meet.

from his neck, was ripped away and left hanging from the branch of a tree. He was dumbstruck, and so terrified that he didn't know what to do. And then, coming up behind him, he heard such a terrible din, such an awesome tumult, that it seemed the whole forest was being torn down in his pursuit, and furious voices were screaming:

'Follow him! Hunt him down! Is he going to escape us?'

Realising his dire plight, Estonné decided he would die but once – and if they pursued him much longer, that death would be soon! So he took his sword in hand and yelled:

'Where are you, then, you pack of screaming demons? Come here and fight, and I'll kill the lot of you!'

Hardly had the words left his lips before he saw dark, shadowy, shapeless figures swirling in the air before him, numerous beyond all counting, and they came shrieking in his face with such hideous and piercing voices that, had he not been so fired with anger, he would surely have lost his mind. But in his rage he dealt such mighty blows with his sword that if the spirits had had mortal bodies he would have cut them to pieces.

And all the while the horse bore him on like the wind, across mountains and deserts, over rivers, through spinneys, accompanied by a noise so great that it seemed the world was about to end. Estonné was soon in such a piteous state, so ripped and torn, so exhausted from hewing at the evil, tormenting spirits, that he was nearly beside himself. His helmet, the laces broken, had been battered back to front by the branches of trees.

At long last, around midnight, the evil spirits stopped plaguing him and the horse came to a halt beside a spring. As soon as Estonné felt the horse pull up he decided to call upon the demon that bore him and ask if he would ever escape the spirits' clutches; but the noise around him was still so great that he doubted he would hear God's thunder. He plucked up courage nonetheless and cried:

'Creature made by the Sovereign Creator, I conjure you by His high power to speak to me – if you're such as can speak to a mortal soul; and if you can't, leave me alone and cease this torment!'

And a spirit inside the horse replied: 'I'm a creature well able to speak to you! What do you want to say to me?'

'I command you,' said Estonné, 'by the power of the Sovereign God who made you, to tell me what manner of thing you are!'

'You summon me,' said the voice, 'by so high a bidding that I must obey. Know, then, that I am one of the angels cast out of Paradise with Lucifer because in his pride he wanted to reign and set himself in competition with God, denying Him the obedience he owed. This caused a great rift in Heaven; but when that God who later made the world saw the outrage committed by Lucifer in his pride, He turned him from the most beautiful angel in Paradise into the ugliest creature that could ever be, and flung him as far from Him as possible – into Hell, which lies in the centre of the Earth, where he must stay, unable ever to come near God. That's why the saying goes that there is no journey as long or barrier as great as exist between Lucifer and God.'

'So how do you come to be here?' asked Estonné. 'How are you this much closer to God than the centre of the Earth?'

'I'll tell you,' the voice replied. 'God is the fairest of judges, and punishes a soul only according to his misdeed. It's only right that the originator and source of wrong should be punished more than a follower. And his closest, keenest followers are those most harshly punished.'

The voice was that of a spirit who could no longer dwell near God but had no wish to be any nearer Lucifer. Estonné asked the source of his mysterious powers.

'They come from God,' the voice replied, 'who allows me to torment creatures for their misdeeds. I love mocking and playing tricks on people like you! But that's as far as my power goes.'

'Well I command you,' said Estonné, 'by the power of the one who condemned you to the torment that you earned, to keep your promise: you told me that if I mounted this horse you'd deliver Branius's castle to me.'

'I'm bound to that promise, truly,' said the voice, 'and I'll fulfil it to the best of my powers.'

Without another word the horse set off at lightning speed the same way it had come, so fast indeed that Estonné didn't know whether he was riding on earth or air.

Thanks to the spirit the castle is taken; but Count Le Tor's campaign in the 'Selve Carbonneuse' is not yet complete: one castle, Falmar, is still held against him and proves even harder to take.

But the besiegers passed their time pleasantly enough in hunting, and it was while he was hunting one day that Estonné found himself in a great expanse of marsh. The marsh reminded him of the demon he'd ridden[6] which had helped him to capture Branius's castle. And he remembered the lovely girl, Sorence by name, whom he'd found asleep in bed after he'd killed Branius in the garden where the demon set him down; and his body grew hot at the thought of how beautiful he'd found her and of the pleasure he'd had with her. He made up his mind to return to her as he'd promised; he abandoned his hunting at once and returned to camp, where he asked Le Tor's leave to go back to Branius's castle. Then he set off, all alone.

After a few days' ride he came one evening within half a league of the castle, and began to sing at the thought of seeing Sorence again. And when he found himself in the meadow just outside he started singing all the more lustily, his heart fired with joy. But when he came to the end of his song he heard a beast making a hideous braying like a donkey – much to his annoyance: he was sure it was done in mockery. He rode ahead, determined to find the beast and give it a good thrashing, and there in the twilight he saw a creature looking something like a bear; he raised his lance and went to hit it with the shaft, but in mid-swing the beast vanished and the blow flashed down to the ground, with such force that the lance broke in two. Estonné was distraught and said he'd be in a fix if a knight challenged him to joust. And just as he said this he looked across the meadow and saw the creature prancing around kicking its legs in the air, and he spurred his horse after it and drew his sword, vowing to take revenge. But when the beast heard him coming it took to its heels, and Estonné chased after as fast as he could. The creature fled into marshy ground, and before Estonné knew it his horse had plunged in a muddy hole and was sinking in right up to its belly. In moments Estonné found himself standing, both feet on the ground, with his horse down below between his legs. Estonné was horrified, and started pulling at his horse's tail to drag it from the mud. But it was no use: the more the horse floundered the deeper it sank. Soon Estonné was so caked in filth that he was unrecognisable; he was nearly demented with rage, and swore that anyone who fell in love was mad, and that if he ever

i.e. because it was in a marsh that he'd first encountered him.

got out of this bog he'd go no further on that maiden's account: she could go to the Devil! And just as he said this, he heard a maiden's voice, somewhere in the distance beyond the swamp, sweetly saying:

'Don't be angry, Estonné: come to me and I'll make everything better!'

He stopped and listened and heard the same words again; he stood there, covered in slime, nonplussed, sure that it was Sorence, the maiden for whose sake he'd come. He started regretting what he'd said, and set off in the direction of the voice, forgetting all about his horse left thrashing in the mud. And with every step he could hear the voice saying:

'Come quickly, my love! My arms are waiting to embrace you!'

He hurried to the meadow where the maiden was, and said: 'Sorence, are you there? You called me!'

'Yes!' the maiden replied. 'Follow me!'

And she headed for a tree at the far end of the meadow.

'What?' said Estonné. 'Can't you wait for me? You can see I've got covered in mud for your sake!'

'Sir,' she said, 'just follow me to this tree, and if I don't then do whatever you want you can say you've been deceived!'

Estonné said no more and went after the girl, not daring to upset her. And when she reached the tree she turned to him and said:

'Sir, I don't want you to take me for a liar, so here I am: I'm all yours!'

Estonné was so thrilled at this that he forgot all his troubles. He threw himself forward, arms outstretched, hot, afire, ready to embrace her; but just as he was about to take her in his arms he saw her face in the light of the moon: it was jaundiced, grizzled, old and wrinkled, with sagging cheeks, shrivelled lips and a sunken nose – an uglier, more deformed thing was never seen by man! And in a coarse and quavering voice the old crone said:

'Get away, Sir Filthy Vagrant! Don't come near me till you've washed yourself in the river and put on some decent clothes! How dare you come to me in that state?'

Estonné went crazy – he couldn't help himself – and cried: 'You foul, crabby hag! Hellfire seize you before I do!'

And cursing the false allure of loving women he drew his sword and struck out at the crone with all his force as she stood leaning against the tree; but she vanished, and the sword plunged into the trunk, so deeply that he couldn't pull it out.

Estonné berated himself for having not followed his first decision to be done with the girl and forget her. 'How ever did you come to love her? Who put it in your head?' And he weighed the trials and tribulations of love with the pleasures that it gave and 'if you thought how short-lived the pleasures are you'd never tolerate the trials! You'd wait for the woman to come to you!' And he stood there, covered in mud from head to foot, and wondered what Sorence would think if she saw him. 'She wouldn't dare to say it, but she'd mock you in her heart!'

Just then he saw a light moving along the castle wall, and decided to go and find help to get his horse out of the bog: he'd no intention of going further – all he wanted to do was ride back and rejoin the siege of Falmar. But as he approached the light he heard a maiden singing on the battlements of the main tower, and in the moonlight he saw it was Sorence relaxing in the calm of the evening and he recognised her voice. He thought how craven it would be to leave without speaking to that lovely girl – what a disgrace it would be if anyone knew! – and he shouldn't be so easily dispirited, and no man had a right to enjoy the pleasure of a lady if he hadn't the heart to suffer a little hardship to win such incomparable joy! So he went after the light and called to its carrier to show him into the castle.

'Follow, follow,' came the reply, 'and you'll soon be inside!'

So Estonné followed, and found himself in the town. It was late, and few people were out of doors. And few were his steps before the light led him to a midden. Then the light vanished and Estonné went tumbling into all the filth and dung and was befouled by the dark, disgusting ooze. There's no need to ask if he was angry! He staggered up and heaped curses on every god he believed in, and said, loud enough for a girl at a nearby window to hear:

'Damn Sorence and every woman in the world! Look what she's made me suffer!'

The girl heard this and came straight back with: 'What's your problem with women? Damn you, sir! From what you say, they must have given you their love too cheaply, if you curse them just because you've got a bit wet! It doesn't take much to make you give up on a worthy affair! You'd better take care of what honour you have, for you won't win much more – you're such a delicate thing!' Estonné was horrified by her words; but the girl came down and stood before him and took him by the hand and said: 'Don't worry, sir knight. I know you – I've seen you before. Be comforted: before tomorrow's dawn there'll be something to make you forget you fell in a midden!'

And she led him into the house and washed him and dressed him in fresh clothes. She'd called for Sorence, and she came. When Estonné saw her he was so happy that he forgot everything that had happened. And after their joyful exchange of greetings, the girl told Sorence how Estonné had cursed her – and all women on her account – and the reason why.

'Damsel,' said Estonné, 'there are rather more reasons than that!' And he told her all the mishaps that had befallen him on the way.

'Sir,' said Sorence, 'it's discourteous of you to lay the blame on me and other women – and quite wrong: lay the blame on your master Zephir, who carries you back and forth as you wish.'

'What, damsel? Who's my master Zephir?'

'The horse,' she replied, 'who carried you to Branius's tower. You would never have taken it – or me! – if it hadn't been for him.'

'By my father's soul,' said Estonné, 'I never thought of him! Though he told me he liked nothing so much as tricking people!'

'Don't be surprised that he tricked you, sir,' said Sorence. 'Everyone in this city knows Zephir and his pranks: he catches out even the sharpest! They're on their guard from dusk to midnight – that's when his powers are at their height – so watch out for him another time.'

'How shall I do that?'

'I don't really know!' she said. 'He shifts his shape in so many ways and changes the sound of his voice so much that I can't suggest anything useful! But if he plays another trick on you, the best thing to do is just laugh!'

Troylus in love

If ever a chivalric romance asserted the inspirational effects of women — and of love itself — upon a knight, it is Perceforest. All people, the author makes plain, should be subjects of the lord Love, and if they've yet to pay him homage they have no meaningful place in the world. And if we're not inspired by our commitment to that mighty lord, how much, the author asks, are we ever likely to achieve? This idea is explored wittily — but with no lack of serious intent — when the great knight Lyonnel du Glat, who has been achieving extraordinary feats for the love of his beloved Blanchete, meets a former companion while on his way to a tournament.

Lyonnel was overjoyed to meet Troylus again, and he told him he'd been well rewarded for everything he'd endured in his adventures with the lions, the serpent and the giant. He would undertake any challenge, he said, no matter how much suffering was involved, 'to earn half the reward I've had for this!'

'Then your prize, sir,' said Troylus, 'has been rich indeed! Is the prize in gold? Or in castles or cities?'

'What do you mean, sir?' Lyonnel replied. 'You think you can compare my reward to gold or cities? If you were as rich as Alexander ever was and you offered to bequeath me all your wealth in exchange for my reward I wouldn't accept — no, I wouldn't exchange it for all the Earth!'

'Then I take it your prize isn't worldly?'

'Oh Troylus,' said Lyonnel, 'it's worldly, yes, made of flesh and bone, and given life by the Sovereign God. But it's no ordinary piece of work! Never has Nature created a girl of such perfect beauty as the one I beheld for my reward.' The sight of her had been, he said, an unprecedented inspiration to him, filling his heart with the desire to achieve feats of all possible honour, nobility and prowess. 'How could the riches of Alexander and all the lands he conquered ever compare with that?'

Troylus agreed, but said that he, too, had been given by God a great desire to win honour; and he wondered whether 'if I fell in love with a noble maiden of good name, would it make me a better knight?'

'You mean you're not in love?' said Lyonnel.

'Well, sir, I can't say I hate anyone, but there's no lady or maiden I love more than any other.'

'Then truly,' Lyonnel said, 'you're of far less honour and prowess, and I can't believe you'd be able to achieve any great feats of arms! Indeed, all those who are truly in love would be tarnished by your company – and since I can do without being tarnished, I renounce it!'

'What, sir!' said Troylus. 'You renounce my company because I'm not in love?' And then, realising Lyonnel was in earnest, he said: 'I vow to the god of Love I'll never drink anything but water till I have a sweetheart!'

Lyonnel accepted his good intentions and set off with him, praying that 'the Sovereign God may send you a sweetheart of such goodness, worth and beauty that you may grow in prowess and honour!'

Then, on the fourth day of their journey to Neuf Chastel, they encountered six knights drinking and washing at a spring. They were instantly challenged to joust, and Lyonnel, not wanting to use the shields and lances that he'd promised to bear at the tournament, said to Troylus: 'You'll have to handle this – but no! Lend me your shield and lance and I'll do it: I'm worried about you, not being in love!'

'You're quite wrong, sir!' said Troylus. 'We can't all be as lucky as you, finding someone to fall in love with; but as you know, I've promised to join your order as soon as Love will have me, so now we'll see what'll happen on the basis of my promise!'

Unhorsing the first knight with a mighty blow, Troylus rode back to Lyonnel and said: 'Well sir, what do you think? Has my willingness to make up for disgracefully being without a sweetheart for so long counted in my favour?'

'Sir,' said Lyonnel, 'even the greatest sinner can be forgiven if he repents! So you'd better repent the time you've lost and defend yourself against the other knight that's coming!'

Troylus brilliantly toppled the second knight, too, and Lyonnel cried: 'Ah, Troylus, what a great knight you'd be if you were in love!'

'I have to say, sir,' said Troylus, 'you puzzle me. You're convinced no one can be any good unless he's in love. I'm not talking about myself – I don't consider myself of great worth – but I can think of many knights of great prowess who've never been in love.'

'Nonsense!' said Lyonnel. 'No knight can be of great prowess if he hasn't truly loved! If they pull off the odd feat it's just by chance – or because they've been dealing with knights who're not in love!' As he said this Lyonnel looked up and saw another knight charging forward to joust, and he pointed him out to Troylus, saying: 'Get ready – you've got to joust again. Just keep thinking of the god of Love and you'll be all right!'

Troylus brought down the third and a fourth straight after. Up came a fifth, and again Lyonnel called out to Troylus to 'pray to the god of Love to help you!'

'Sir,' he replied, 'do you really think I'm that forgetful? You're reminding me about Love so much that I can think of nothing else!'

And he met the knight with such a blow that he bore him to the ground with his horse on top of him. Forward came the sixth and last knight, praising him for toppling his five companions but vowing to avenge them. Seeing how young this sixth knight was, Troylus warned him not to joust; but the young knight replied that, despite his youth, 'I hope to gain revenge with the help of Love! I wish the maiden I adore were here now to see my first joust!'

When Lyonnel heard the bold words of the young knight resting his hope on Love he was alarmed for Troylus, and came to him and said: 'Dear friend, I'm a bit worried about you fighting this young knight: he's in love and you're not! Lend me your shield and lance and I'll take him on.'

Troylus took offence at this. 'By God, sir, no you won't! I'm going to finish this business!'

'Oh sir!' cried Lyonnel. 'Then remember Love, I beg you! I fear for you: you haven't paid Him homage yet!'

'Honestly!' Troylus hotly replied. 'You've gone on and on about your god of Love, but it's not going to make me give up this joust! I've brought down five knights today, the least of them twice as strong as this youth! So I'll bring him down, too, if God means me to!'

'But the five knights you toppled weren't in love!'

'Weren't in love?' said Troylus, angry now. 'How can you possibly know?'

'Don't get annoyed – you should be grateful for the advice. I tell you, no knight like you who's not in love could have brought down five knights as good as these if they were!'

'I think you and other lovers,' said the irritated Troylus, 'trust too much in love. Don't expect me to! Now come what may!'

And he went charging towards the young knight who, being fired and inspired, wallowing as he was in the hot waters of Love, came straight to meet him, crying: 'Love, be on my side! Oh my sweetheart, why aren't you here?'

And with these words he struck Troylus so hard in the middle of his shield that he brought him and his horse crashing down in a heap. When he saw Troylus down and found himself still in the saddle he was jubilant and yelled:

'Love and my sweetheart, thank you for this triumph! It's through no prowess of mine!'

He challenged Lyonnel to avenge his fallen companion, but Lyonnel declined, saying: 'It's no wonder you beat him with the aid of that lord of yours! But I'm as much his vassal and subject as you are, so out of respect for our lord I'll not joust with you!' He asked the youth his name and learned that he was Zelandin, son of the lord of an isle called Zeeland.

Troylus had got over his upset, realising that being in love had determined the outcome of the joust, and thanked Zelandin for teaching him that 'a knight in search of honour and glory can achieve little unless he's in love.'

'What, sir? You mean you're not?'

'No indeed,' said Troylus. 'But I wish I were.'

'Then I don't consider my victory as great as I did! I thought you must be one of the order when I saw how you dealt with my companions! Obviously the reason you beat them was that they're not in love any more than you are. So it's no wonder I beat you even though you beat them, for a knight without a sweetheart will never beat a knight in love!'

Lyonnel agreed, telling Troylus that 'if you were in love you'd be one of the greatest knights in the world!'

'Sir,' Troylus replied, 'you've told me enough, and I've seen enough of Love's power, to know I'll never be happy till I find a sweetheart!'

The five fallen knights had heard all this, but declared they knew nothing of love and would never meddle in it, for they'd seen so many suffer its misfortunes; and Zelandin dismissed them in disgust, and set off with Lyonnel and Troylus, talking of love the whole way.

A New Order of Chivalry — the 'Franc Palais'

There is a strong possibility that Perceforest inspired the founding of the Order of the Garter by Edward III of England and the Company of the Star by John II of France. King Perceforest's Order of the Franc Palais and the building that housed it are described in the following episode. It begins as Perceforest, triumphantly recovered from his long depression following Alexander's death, is about to celebrate with a great feast and tournament.

Supper had been prepared, spread on tables in a garden below the castle walls, for there were so many people that they couldn't be accommodated in the hall.

While they were seated there at the tables, celebrating as no one in the world had ever done for the return of the king and for the health restored to him, they heard the windows of the great hall slam shut all together with an enormous crash. They wondered what it could mean; and a moment later the windows reopened, and they saw a light shining in the hall as bright as if a hundred torches were blazing. The king asked where such a light could be coming from, and why the windows had closed and reopened; and old Nicorant the castellan said:

'Truly, my lord, I don't know: I've never seen such a thing.'

The king sent him to the hall to investigate, and he came straight back to report a great mystery: 'the doors are locked fast against me, and I can hear a terrible noise of hammering inside, as if it were full of smiths!'

Perceforest listened and heard the hammering and was baffled — as was everyone: no one could explain it. Then, while they were all busy exchanging opinions, they saw a group of twelve maidens pass by, each carrying a shield hung from her neck covered with a green cloth. And truly, they rode straight past the tables without saying a word to any knight or lady. Perceforest wondered what it would all portend, and ordered the castellan to follow them and see where they were going. He set off after them and saw them enter the great hall, whereupon the doors shut fast behind them. He returned to the king and reported what he'd seen, and the king replied:

'There's a meaning to this. God grant that it be to our honour – and the kingdom's!'

Hardly had these words left the king's lips when he looked towards the castle and saw the twelve maidens on their palfreys returning the way they'd come. As they rode back past the tables the king bade the castellan go and ask whose household they were from. He did so, and returned to the king and said:

'They told me it would soon be revealed and that I shouldn't worry about it yet!'

The king decided to forget the matter, not wanting to spoil the feast: he could see that everyone was so keen to celebrate that he would have hated to dampen their spirits. They were served so splendidly that all were more than satisfied, and when the feasting was finally done they rose from the tables and all the knights and ladies began to dance.

Meanwhile the king withdrew with some of his knights and told them he was mystified about the business in the hall, and he took twelve knights, his wife the queen, his sister Fezonas and Edea, and also summoned Sarra and Fraze, Chicora and Falize. Torches were lit and they made their way to the hall.

But when they came to the doorway at the foot of the stairs they found the doors shut tight; then Perceforest looked up and saw written on the arch above, in great and elegant letters of gold, the following:

> 'Let all men know that from this day
> This is the door to the Franc Palais,[7]
> Where honour on the worthy shall be bestowed
> And the worthless shall dishonour know.'

Everyone was astonished: they knew for certain that before sunset no inscription had been there. The king wondered who could have written it so quickly, and he said to Sarra, who was standing beside him:

'I'll swear, damsel, this has been done by magic! I beg you, tell me if you know how this has happened.'

'Truly, my lord,' the lady replied, 'I've no idea. But I do believe it'll be for the greater glory of all chivalry: cowards and sluggards

---

[7]   'Noble Hall'.

will strive to better themselves, and the worthy will find reward and recognition.'

'I hope it proves to be as you say. But come, let's go inside: I long to know if there's some new wonder there.'

So the king stepped forward and told the castellan to let them in. As soon as the doors were open, Perceforest and all his company entered; and once the torches had been placed in the middle they could see the whole hall clearly.

Now, so that you may better understand what we'll tell you in due course, you need to know what the great hall was like. Know, then, that it was on the first floor of a round tower of astounding size: the diameter of the hall was more than two hundred feet. In the centre stood an enormous pillar that supported the vaulted ceiling; inside this pillar was a pipe running from a beautiful spring, and around it were twelve taps providing a constant supply of water. Right round the hall curved a marble table, superbly made, standing quite high off the ground on pillars; and it ran so close to the windows that anyone sitting at the table would be resting his back against the tower wall. The two ends of the table finished in front of the hall's main door, and such was its circumference that it could seat fully three hundred knights abreast.[8] You cannot believe how beautiful this table was to behold, smoother than any ivory. It was impossible to move it, but there were a good many more tables set up in the hall on trestles, so that twelve hundred knights could dine there without impeding the servants.

King Perceforest, at the head of the awestruck party, walked up to the marble table, which was blacker than jet or ink. And he saw that above it were finely made iron hooks, fixed in the wall in careful order all around the hall, numbering in total three hundred or more. The king and all his company wondered what they could be for; then the king looked ahead and at the far end of the great hall, on twelve of the hooks, he saw twelve shields hanging.

[8]   In *The Tournament in England, 1100-1400* (Woodbridge, 1986), Juliet Barker suggests that the 'House of the Round Table' commissioned by Edward III at Windsor Castle in 1344 was 'in direct imitation' [p.93] of the Franc Palais in *Perceforest*. For a detailed discussion of the striking similarities between the description of the Franc Palais and Edward's Round Table House – intended for an order of 300 knights – see J. Munby, R. Barber and R. Brown, *Edward III's Round Table at Windsor* (Woodbridge, 2007), chapter 8, especially pp.106-7.

'Look,' he said. 'Another surprise! Let's go and see what this is about.'

As soon as they reached the shields the queen said: 'These are the shields of the twelve knights who fulfilled their vows to the hermit at the great tournament between Scydrac and Tantalon.'

The king, gazing at them intrigued, replied: 'I'd love to know how they got here.'

'Truly, my lord,' said the castellan, 'I think they're the shields carried by the twelve maidens who passed our tables without speaking: I saw them enter the hall and the doors close behind them.'

'I do believe you're right,' said the king.

While he was talking to the castellan, the queen looked at the marble table and noticed white letters inscribed. She called to the king and said: 'Here's another wonder, my lord!'

The king looked down and saw the letters on the marble, saying:

> 'Pay good heed to this warning:
> No man should sit at this table
> Unless his shield be hung on the hook above –
> If not, I cannot protect him
> From the gravest harm.
> I have no wish to see him in trouble
> And advise him not to sit in any of these seats.
> I hope he will take these words to heart.
> Let him go and sit at the tables below,
> For there he will be safe.'

The king was amazed by these strange words and said: 'It seems to me, sirs, it would be unwise for any knight to sit at the marble table unless his shield is hung above him. It's an inspiration to knights to excel, for I don't think any knight could sit at this table unless he's sufficient in honour and prowess. It seems the time has come when the worthy will receive true recognition; for none should be deemed a knight of excellence unless he has a secure seat at the marble table and his shield is hung from a hook above him here in the Franc Palais. You'll see many knights fighting hard at tomorrow's tournament to win esteem. This new wonder should be made known to all who've gathered here in the hope of honour so that they strive to excel themselves; for when they see what's been instituted here in the hall and the esteem that would be gained by winning a seat at the table, they'll be hungry for such high honour. I declare my wish that henceforth all who by their prowess earn a seat here shall be called Knights of the Franc Palais, in honour and commendation of their chivalry.'

After making this decree, the king told the company that it was time to retire until the morrow, a mighty day of combat between the valiant when they would prove the strength of their arms.

The queen now took the king to bed; she hadn't seen him in such health for eighteen years. Once in bed they abandoned themselves to the joys of love, and little wonder!

When the king rose next morning several of the queen's knights came to him and said: 'We've just come from the great hall, my lord, and you wouldn't believe the throng of knights who've gone to see the marvels!'

'And what are they saying?'

'That any knight whose prowess was such that he could sit at the table would win high honour indeed! The braggarts who're full of talk of how they've won tourneys and achieved great feats are all aghast!'

'Sirs,' said the king, 'I want to go there and see the crowd!'

When he reached the great hall and the throng of knights saw him, they all bowed and made way and said: 'Let's follow the king and hear what he has to say about this wonder!'

The noble king made his way up the stairs and entered the hall, followed by all his knights. And as soon as he entered he looked ahead and saw a group of eight knights marvelling at the letters written on the table and at the twelve shields hanging on the hooks, but treating it all as a joke. One of them jumped on the table and said he'd take one of the shields down; he grabbed the shield with the griffon and tried to unhook it, but he couldn't have moved it an inch for all the gold that would have filled the hall. He was baffled, and said it must be nailed there; but he looked at the wall behind the shield and saw that wasn't the answer. This knight came from an island just off the coast of Britain called the Isle of Vermin; he was lord of the isle and his name was Verminex. He'd told his squire to bring him his own shield, saying he wanted to hang it beside the other twelve, for he was well worthy and had chosen a seat for himself right there. And as soon as he saw his squire coming with his shield, he said to him:

'Give it to me, and I'll hang it beside these others to mark my place.'

So the squire gave him the shield, and Verminex took it and lifted it up, intending to hang it on the hook next to the twelve; but for all his strength he couldn't do it: no matter how he tried to throw the strap over the hook he couldn't make it stay. He kept straining to hang his shield till sweat poured from his brow and he was so exhausted that he had to rest. Then, in a furious temper, he ordered his squire to hang the shield for him. He climbed on to the table and tried to do so, but found it impossible. He was very annoyed, and went round trying every hook in the hall: there were three hundred of them, but he couldn't find a single hook on which he could hang his master's shield.

Then Verminex, realising there was no place for his shield in the hall, spitefully said, like the malicious and resentful soul he was: 'Whether or not my shield has a place here, I'll be the first to sit at the table!'

And a voice rang out from on high and was heard by everyone, saying: 'Then you'll be the first thereby to die!'

And it was true: no sooner had he sat down at the table and ordered his page to bring him food than a hand clutching a sword descended from above and sliced off his head and sent it crashing on to the table before him, and a voice said:

'Now you can eat!'

The king and the throng of knights beheld this awesome sight and were deeply shocked; for a long while no one had the courage to say a word. The king saw their consternation and decided to rouse them from their dismay. So he stepped on to the table and said:

'Sir knights, all of you assembled here, it's been said since ancient times, and will be said evermore, that the easiest way to learn is from another's errors. We should ponder and learn from the example of this knight who's been put to death for his sin. He was the boldest and most valiant knight in his land and, if judged by his prowess, was worthy to have a seat at the table of the Franc Palais and a hook to hang his shield – without which, it appears, no knight can sit there without coming to grief. But I'm reminded of the words of a hermit who warned me once that, even if I possessed all the wealth of King Alexander, all the wisdom of King Solomon and all the chivalry of the valiant Hector of Troy, pride alone, if it reigned in me, would nullify all.

'Sirs,' the king continued, 'this dead knight had wealth and wisdom and chivalry. But pride reigned in him, that's clear, and drove him to covetousness and vanity: wicked covetousness when he senselessly yearned to have the first seat at the table, and vanity when he sat in a place destined for a finer knight than he. And so the Sovereign God wished him to have no seat, high or low. By this example, sir knights, you can see that, no matter how wealthy, wise or strong a knight may be, if he's tainted with vices – especially pride, which leads a man to fall into all the rest – he's not worthy to be called a knight or to sit at the table of the Franc Palais.

'Be assured, sirs, that the knight who is modest and courteous, wise and discreet and armed with virtues, will need fewer deeds of chivalry to reach the high table of the Franc Palais; it's not necessary for every man to be as valiant as Hector of Troy or King Alexander, but it's essential that he be a man of noble qualities. I remember the words of a holy man, who taught me once that knights and clerks should resemble the maid, for the maid should be modest and quiet and composed, courteous, chaste and honest in words and deeds, gentle, good-natured and well-disposed towards the good, and resolute, strong and sharp in response to any who seek to do her wrong. And she should be content with whatever beauty or worldly wealth she may have, and covetous only for acquiring more virtues and doing works pleasing to the Sovereign God.

'If they want to perfect the role to which they're committed, knights and clerks should resemble the maid in all respects. For the clerk who follows vice and turns his back on virtue is no clerk at all. No matter that he's acquired enough knowledge to be named a clerk: the vices in him deprive him of that name and place in the brotherhood; for a fine white sheet is more shamefully stained by a single drop of blood than coarse cloth dragged through a dung-heap!

'And the same is true for you, sir knights; for if one who has received the order of knighthood fails to resemble the maid in graces and virtues, he has no right to be called a knight, however valiant he may be. If one man says: "He's a good, bold and valiant knight" but another replies: "He's ruthless and haughty and spiteful towards the poor and those below him, false and insincere in word and deed, lewd and full of vices", then he's not worthy to be a knight. Even if it's true that he's valiant and bold, it's sheer mischance and against what Nature intended that any prowess should be found in him, and he shouldn't enjoy any praise or respect.

'All who have seats at the table and their shields hung on the hooks above shall be named Knights of the Franc Palais. And my wish is that henceforth ladies and damsels, maids, widows and orphans, knights and anyone in distress should appeal and have recourse to the Franc Palais, and that all the knights of the table shall be bound to give them aid and guidance in any just quarrel.

'And I pray also that any knights who, through some failing, do not achieve this high honour as soon as they would wish, should not be angry and impatient, but determined to better themselves by pursuing prowess and chivalry in all matters so that, by their improvement, they may sooner attain this high honour. And because I wish it to be revealed without dispute which knights shall be worthy to sit at the table of the Franc Palais, I command all who wish to compete in today's tournament and attain this high honour to have one of their shields brought here to the hall – as I shall bring my own – and then the hall shall be locked; for such is my faith in the power of the Sovereign God that I believe that, at the dinner after the tournament, those who are worthy will find their shields hung on the hooks, and thereby know where they are to sit.

'And I command that the head of the knight who was killed here for his sin shall be hung on a chain from the ceiling of the hall, as a reminder that henceforth no man should be so presumptuous as to sit at the table unless his shield be hung above his seat. Go now, sirs, and make your preparations. And order your lives: be like the maid and worthy of the name of knight, so that you may sit at the noble table of the Franc Palais for the rest of your life, and end it at the table of the Sovereign God in His Paradise. Amen.'

When the noble King Perceforest had finished his sermon he stepped down from the table, and the knights who'd gathered in the hall began to file out, praising and thanking the noble king for having taught them what they needed to do if they aspired to honour.

Later that day the tournament raged until more than two hundred knights lay strewn about the field, exhausted. But the flower of the tournament, still fighting, were so hotly engaged that it seemed like mortal battle, and King Perceforest decided to call a halt before there were any deaths. He came down from the stand and mounted his horse and rode into the mêlée, silver mace in hand, and commanded them to stop. Then the chief herald announced to all to come to supper in the Franc Palais, where rewards would be distributed according to deserts.

Soon a great throng had assembled outside the great hall, all desperate to know if they would be honoured with a place at the table. Finally the king commanded that the doors be opened, and the great crowd entered in awed and reverent silence.

Inside, in the middle of the hall, they found thirty-two trestle tables radiating outward from the hall's central pillar; but the great circular table that ran around the wall was two feet higher than these, and covered with the richest cloths. The king looked up at the hooks on the wall; only sixty-three of them bore shields. These sixty-three by their great prowess had earned a seat at the noble table of the Franc Palais. The shields of those not worthy of places were arrayed along the thirty-two lower tables.

'My lords,' the king said, 'we should indeed worship the Sovereign God, who has established and arranged this hall in such a way that each man, without quarrel or dispute or question, is assigned a seat according to his worth.' And he bade them all sit in the places marked by their shields, and avoid the death that Verminex had brought upon himself by his presumption.

The God of the Sheer Mountain

The author's attitude to magic is ambiguous. The Fairy Queen, King Gadifer's wife, uses her skills in magic to manifestly good ends: she gives her son, young Gadifer, a magic ring that enables him to see through any illusion; and her knowledge of what the stars and planets predestine helps her to save her sons from wounds they deal each other with their lances. Magic — acquiring and using knowledge of nature's workings — is not, the author implies, in itself a bad thing; but what is to be avoided, he says, is for a 'magician' to become adept and imagine he's therefore godlike. In the following episode, young Gadifer has responded to a plea by a maiden named Pierote to undertake a mysterious mission; it leads him to encounter the enchanter Aroés, who has set himself up as God of the Sheer Mountain.

The master mariner was awestruck to hear that such a young knight as Gadifer had undertaken the mission to the kingdom of the Sheer Mountain.

'Do you know what the adventure entails?' he asked him.

'I know nothing about it, truly,' Gadifer replied. 'The maiden Pierote died before she could tell me what I was engaged to do.'

'I know nothing, either!' the mariner said. 'Nor do I see how you can enter the kingdom from any direction! It's a mountain about a hundred leagues in circumference, and on every side it soars sheer to the height of a bowshot: no bird can even find a perch! And the sea has worn away the land all round and pounds at its foot on every side. The sovereign king of the land is a god named Aroés; and his power is such that he heals his subjects of all sickness, and when he chooses that they should die he carries them to his holy paradise which lies in the air at the heart of his kingdom. And this god is so feared in these parts that, even if the mountain were more accessible than it is, no man would dare to enter the realm without his leave for fear of instant death.'

But Gadifer was unafraid. 'I'd have trouble achieving anything worthwhile if I was daunted by what men say!'

They sailed night and day until they found themselves close to the Sheer Mountain. It was indeed a forbidding sight, and Gadifer was dismayed and asked the mariner: 'Master, is this mountain equally hard to climb on every side?'

'Indeed it is, sir!' he replied.

'Then how do you trade with the island?'

'I'll tell you,' said the mariner. 'Whenever they need merchandise, they send someone like poor Pierote down in a machine, and then I take them aboard and return them once their errand's done, and the machine carries them back up with whatever they've bought. I've two big parcels on board now – one for the god Aroés and the other for the queen – and before nightfall you'll see them hauled to the top of the mountain.'

'Very interesting,' said Gadifer. 'I'll have to think about that!' And Gadifer conceived a plan. He asked the mariner to stow him inside one of the parcels 'so that no one sees me till it's untied!'

The mariner was appalled: had he no fear of death? 'If you were caught up there they'd kill you, even if you had as many lives as the population of mighty Troy!'

'When I'm dead,' Gadifer replied, 'mankind will only be reduced by one, and he's of little worth! Do as I ask.'

So the mariner took Gadifer over to the bundles, one of which was full of herbs and powders and other strange things with which the god Aroés cast spells on all the people of his realm, and the other, the queen's, was full of fine silk and linen. He asked him which he'd prefer to hide in, and Gadifer replied that he'd rather fall into the hands of women than men, and so preferred to be stowed in the parcel for the queen.

The mariner hid Gadifer in the bundle with just enough air to breathe. Then he signalled to watchmen in the castle, high up on the brink of the mountain's sheer side, and they lowered their machine. He loaded it with the package for the god Aroés, who was more than pleased to receive his bundle for he needed its contents urgently, and he had it carried to the study where he worked his spells, and shut himself inside to see to his business.

Meanwhile his daughter Flamine gave orders for her mother the queen's package to be hauled to the mountain top. But she was surprised when Pierote didn't appear with the bundle and, with an anguished heart, said:

'Ah, Pierote, dear friend! Why have you not returned with these goods after being away so long? You clearly couldn't find help at the court of King Perceforest, where my mother placed all her hope! She kept warning me I was doomed unless I was rescued by some knight of that noble king's line! Now I'm lost for sure, for my mother's been taken from me, and she was my only support and refuge! Truly, Pierote, if you've failed to return now, there's no hope of your being back in time: I've only two days' respite before I'm compelled to do what is forbidden in all laws. It would have been better if I'd died on the day I was born than be forced to such foulness!'

Gadifer heard every word of this and couldn't contain himself. Sensing she was alone in her chamber, he decided to speak up there and then. 'Untie me, girl!' he said. 'Your help is here!'

She was astonished to hear the man's voice inside the bundle. 'Who's that in there?'

'The rescuer Pierote came to find in England!'

Flamine was unconvinced, and afraid it might be the voice of some ungodly creature; but Gadifer said: 'I'm a knight of the Franc Palais, of which King Perceforest is the sovereign lord. You're safe to untie me – have no fear!'

Reassured by this she opened the bundle and found inside a fully armed knight, shield on chest, sword in hand and helmet laced, and terrified by the sight she cried: 'Almighty God! How did this knight get here?'

'Damsel,' said Gadifer, 'I came at your command!'

And he stood up and removed his helm; and when she saw him standing there, so handsome and young, she flushed as red as any rose. For a moment he stood looking at her in silence, and thought he'd never seen a lovelier girl of her age – she was only about fifteen; and she, blushing as she gazed at him, thought she'd never seen a knight of more handsome face and body.

Seeing her embarrassment, Gadifer broke the silence and explained how he'd come to be there: how, newly knighted, he'd responded to Pierote's appeal to Perceforest's court and undertaken the unknown mission to the Sheer Mountain. Flamine wept when he spoke of Pierote's death, and told Gadifer that her mother the queen had also died. And now at last he discovered exactly why his help was needed, as she said:

'King Aroés, lord of this mountain, used his magic to abduct my mother from the White Island, of which she'd been the lady after the death of her father and mother; he took her as his wife, whether she liked it or not, and upon her sired a daughter whom you see before you now. When my mother came of age and realised what kind of life my father led – and understood the difference between right and wrong – she told herself that the Sovereign God would not long tolerate her husband's actions, and she was afraid of being an accomplice. Through divination she discovered that this mountain would crumble into an abyss because of her husband's foul sin and all the kingdom's people would be damned; she was horrified, and couldn't think what to do for the best. And further divination told her that my father Aroés would kill her in the end and take me as his wife – with no regard for the sin! – unless he was prevented by a British knight of King Perceforest's blood.'

And now Flamine told Gadifer of her father's wicked ways. 'Ever since he was a child he's been the most skilled magician in these parts. He became so adept at sorcery that his pride became overweening: he gave no thought to the Sovereign God and insisted he was God himself, for if he hadn't been God omnipotent he couldn't have done what he did! He told his people he could protect them from all other gods and cure them of all sickness, and if they worshipped him as the Sovereign God he would grant them a painless death when their time came and a place in his holy paradise, which he would establish at the heart of the kingdom so that four times a year they could go and see the souls of their dead mothers and fathers and kinsmen in everlasting glory. And he did indeed establish a hospital where he performed instant cures upon many who became mysteriously sick; but there was another side to it: all who became ill by natural causes and wouldn't recover within a week he had taken by night and thrown from a window into the sea, and then had an accomplice allege that they'd wanted to die, and that he'd taken them to his paradise!

'Then a day came when he told his people to gather to see all the souls of their dead relations. They assembled in the place of his supposed paradise, known as the Holy March, but saw nothing in the air or on the ground till dusk, when a mysterious and unnerving light appeared, followed by a vision in the air of a circular palace of astounding size, with windows all the way round, and lit within by a dazzling light. It seemed to be made of pure gold, inside and out. Everyone stood in stunned silence, till suddenly they heard ravish-

ing, glorious music playing inside the palace, and a vast number of
souls in the shapes of men and women appeared at the windows, all
dancing joyously; and Aroés could be seen inside, sitting on a jew-
elled throne in majesty, the apparent source of all the radiant light.
The people watching were overwhelmed, convinced they recognised
the souls of fathers, mothers, sisters; and they declared to Aroés that:
"Anyone who fails to worship you as the sovereign god above all
others is mad!" He told them he'd now demonstrated the truth of
his claims and promises, but warned them that, if they displeased or
opposed him, he was equally capable of inflicting pain and tribula-
tion, making them suffer an agonising death and sending them to his
hell! They asked him to show them this hell, so that they'd understand
what torments would be in store for any who failed to worship him.
He was offended by this, and said: "It seems you want to tempt and
test me! You obviously doubt my word! This insolence comes from
my familiarity: it's said by the wise that no prophet is accepted in
his own country!" He told them to gather in the same place a month
later; then the paradise disappeared.

'He worked busily with his spells and conjurations, and when the
people reassembled at the month's end the vision of paradise reap-
peared with Aroés at the windows announcing that he would show
them "the place where the wicked will be punished everlastingly, especially those who refuse to believe in me!" Suddenly the people
were plunged into total darkness, and heard terrible rumblings beneath the earth and human voices wailing and howling in pain; then
a terrifying abyss yawned before them from which belched an appalling smoke, so dense with the stench of sulphur that it seemed it
was meant to break the strongest hearts in the world; and in its midst
they could see souls being hung, roasted, boiled, torn and broken on
wheels. When the vision finally dissolved and they could see Aroés in
his glorious paradise once more, the people declared their total devo-
tion to him, their only possible saviour from those monstrous torments. In their deluded state they considered themselves the luckiest
people in the world, and called that place the Field of Joy.

'And now my father believes he's immortal, and thinks he'll soon
be worshipped as the sovereign god throughout the world! And when
my mother the queen fell ill, she was terrified that if she didn't recover in a week he would have her thrown in the sea, for she was

growing old and losing her beauty and he was lusting after me! And remembering the prediction – that he would kill her and marry me, his daughter – my mother sent Pierote on her quest for help, for she'd seen through divination that if she died but I could be rescued, then before two days had passed this mountain would split in four and crumble into an abyss with my father and his people. And she warned me: "Don't give in to your father's wicked demands – whatever promises or threats he makes – for if you consent you're sure to be swallowed up in Hell with him and his accomplices!"

'Within a week my mother was dead as she'd predicted, and my father came and told me: "On her deathbed what grieved your mother most was that she was leaving me without a wife, for she could think of no one worthy of me. But I promised out of love for her to take you as my wife – as I can, being the sovereign god I am! This put her mind completely at rest and she asked me to let her die and take her to my holy paradise. So I had her die then painlessly, and my celestial ministers were there and carried her away to glory. So your mother's death is a great blessing for you! You're to be wife to the almighty god Aroés!"

'I trembled in every limb, and when my father asked me what was wrong I said I thought myself unworthy, and needed a month's respite to prepare myself. This he granted – but now the dreadful day is almost here!'

As Flamine came to the end of her story she collapsed, weeping, in Gadifer's lap; and he, too, wept for pity – so much so that soon he'd soaked her wimple till it clung to her bare and lily-white skin. Then he vowed to save her from her imminent peril 'if the body of a single knight can rescue you; and I'll take you to a safe place and guard your honour as if you were my sister.'

She was much comforted by this, and when he told her he was the son of the king of Scotland, in whom her mother's divination had placed such faith, she gave thanks to the Sovereign God for sending her a knight from such a noble source. She said that, with Pierote dead, there was only one maid she could trust – 'she has no more faith in my father than in a sheep!' And they enlisted the help of this girl, Sorette, to hide Gadifer that night from the evil king.

Next day Sorette helped him arm and then covered him in a cloak of the kind worn in that country. And while Flamine was led in a great procession to the field where she was to marry her father in his paradise, Gadifer followed, hidden in the crowd.

Soon a vast number had gathered, all seated on the ground and gazing into the air, waiting for the paradise to appear. Gadifer saw Flamine sitting by an oak tree and went as close to her as he dared and said:

'Sister, when are we going to see this paradise you've talked about?'

'Quite soon, brother, but it never appears till evening when it grows dark so that his enchantments can be better seen.'

'Tell me then,' said Gadifer, 'is your father in this round tower I see?'

'What, sir?' said Flamine. 'Can you see a tower?'

'Ah, sister!' he said. 'The people of the kingdom are deceived! There's a tower right here, wrapped by magic in thick air that blocks the sight of you and others!'[9]

At that moment the paradise suddenly appeared, with Aroés sitting in dazzling majesty and his dead queen apparently at his side, shining like crystal. Even Flamine, aware now that it was an illusion, was staggered to see her. But while the people gasped at the sight of their "sovereign goddess" and of their fathers, mothers, sisters and brothers, Gadifer was baffled, for he saw nothing of this: all he could see was the bright light of torches blazing high atop a tower and, as he told the bewildered Flamine, 'a knight sitting on a splendid chair in the middle of a vaulted room! I'm going straight up there to see what's going on!'

Flamine was terrified, but Gadifer refused to be daunted. He strode towards the tower and climbed from floor to floor till he found himself at the top where Aroés was creating his wicked illusions. And when he came to the door of the room beneath the roof he saw Aroés sitting on a chair bedecked with flasks full of liquid. There were windows right round that floor of the tower – it was like a round hall – and encircling the room, in front of the windows, was a huge iron ring suspended on wires from the vaulted ceiling. It was hung in such a way that Aroés could make it turn exactly as he pleased at

---

[9]   Gadifer is protected from illusions by a magic ring given to him by his mother the Fairy Queen.

the touch of a finger; and from the ring were hung so many glass phials that Gadifer couldn't count them all, and all were filled with strange liquids made by Aroés's dark arts. And when the light of the torches that blazed around the enchanter shone through these phials, the crowd watching below thought they could see the souls of their families and loved ones. And that wasn't all: the flasks that surrounded Aroés's chair appeared to be minstrels playing all manner of instruments; and there were little glass birds dotted all around, likewise filled with strange liquid, and the watchers below thought they heard birdsong mixed with the music in a harmony that ravished the mind. And Gadifer saw how Aroés had hung a long glass phial beside him, magically empowered to create the image of the queen. Gadifer watched, astounded, as the wicked enchanter rose from his seat and reached beneath his mantle and held up two crystal figures, one in each hand, and all those vulnerable to his magic thought they saw four souls, radiant as the sun, acting as his attendants and spreading his mantle wide. And he came to the window and addressed the crowd, promising them once more the joys and glory of paradise if they would believe in him and worship him, and bidding them all attend his marriage next day to his daughter Flamine.

Gadifer could take no more. He strode forward and cried: 'You're a mortal man as I am! A poor creature made of the four elements by the wisdom of the Sovereign Creator! You've forgotten and lost all sight of Him, foully deceived by the Devil's art! How dare you claim to be a god? You're nothing more than earth and food for worms!'

Aroés was intent upon his sorcery and, in his pride, didn't deign to reply; but he was so incensed that his face blazed and his eyes burned in his head like candle-flames. And in his rage he cast a spell designed to rob the knight of speech and motion.

But Gadifer was ready for this and said: 'Don't waste your time casting spells on me: they can do me no harm!'

When Aroés saw his spell have no effect he was appalled, and asked Gadifer who he was.

'A mortal man like you!' he replied. 'I've come to see you in all your wickedness because I heard you were God omnipotent! But I find you a slave of the Devil, toiling and labouring with your spells and charms to deceive yourself first of all and then your people, commanding them to worship you as the Sovereign God – you who are the most wicked of the whole wretched crew! Take arms and fight, for I'll kill you now unless you recognise your Creator!'

But Aroés retorted that fighting was beneath an omnipotent god like him; instead 'I'll have you torn apart by the demons at my command!'

And he conjured up a band of demons: a diabolical noise surged up around the tower – it seemed it was about to crumble into an abyss; and at Aroés's command they advanced on Gadifer to tear him limb from limb. But they couldn't get within nine feet of him and turned to Aroés, bewildered.

Gadifer mocked him all the more, saying: 'Powerless creature that you are, you had to summon aid! Claim no more to be omnipotent: you can do nothing! What little power you have comes from the Sovereign God, who'll rescue the people of your kingdom from your enslavement, as He freed the children of Israel from the hands of King Pharaoh of Egypt!'

Aroés was outraged. 'How dare you say I'm not the sovereign god, when you see I can summon the princes of darkness by a single word of command?'

'It's through no power of yours,' said Gadifer. 'It's solely through the power with which God has imbued the words you used to call them.'

And with that Gadifer drew his sword and strode across the room, smashing the magic phials and sending them shattering over the floor as he headed for Aroés. The enchanter appealed in desperation to the evil spirits, and they surrounded him and bore him through a window and away into the air, with such a monstrous howling din that it seemed the world was about to end.

Many of the people were so terrified that they fled into the forest, thinking something had happened to displease their god; but as Gadifer smashed the last of the phials and completely broke the enchanter's spell, in the light of the moon his paradise was revealed to the rest of the crowd in its true guise of the tower. But still they didn't understand: they thought some strange new god was trying to drive Aroés from his kingdom, and that Aroés had suddenly used his power to build this tower to resist his enemy; and imagining the other god had flown away in the commotion they'd just heard, they decided to guard the tower against attack, thinking Aroés was still inside. They were sure he would ward off attacks from the air and the sky, of which he was the supreme master.

Meanwhile Gadifer slipped from the tower, wrapped in his cloak again, and made his way to the terrified Flamine and Sorette. He told them to fear nothing but to follow him to the sea, saying: 'We must leave the mountain as fast as we can: the demons have carried your father away, but I don't know where.'

They hurried back to the castle, arriving just before dawn, and Flamine told the men who tended the machine that: 'My father Aroés says you're to send down two bundles of goods that Sorette will bring you – and make sure they don't fall in the sea!' Then she went to her chamber, where she and Sorette hid Gadifer in one bundle and Sorette hid her in the other. Both were safely lowered along with Sorette and taken aboard the waiting ship, where Sorette untied them and they gave thanks to the Sovereign Creator for their escape.

But as they celebrated they suddenly saw Aroés on the mountain top; and to their horror he used his evil spells to raise the most terrible storms in the sky and the sea that the mariner had ever seen: thunder, lightning and balls of fire came crashing from the sky. They weighed anchor and put out to sea, and as the ship pulled away from the mountain the storm began to abate. But when they looked back they saw the whole mountain, vast as it was, shrouded in a dense black cloud. It was appalling, monstrous; they'd never seen such a thing; they thought they were doomed, seeing the catastrophe about to hit the mountain. Even the mariner, who'd been through many a squall and tempest, was aghast and said to Gadifer:

'I've sailed the seas for sixty years or more and never seen such a storm brewing; I can't believe it's natural or governed by the planets.'

'I know exactly where it's coming from,' Gadifer replied, 'and what will come of it! Let's wait here awhile, I pray you, and see it through to the end.'

Flamine couldn't bear to look, and buried her head in Gadifer's lap. But he and the sailors watched as the cloud above the mountain grew ever thicker; and in great, fiery whirlwinds they saw a horde of demons in fearsome battle with each other and with the cloud itself. And they saw four demons carrying – as if on a table – an armed knight who was standing up with shield slung from neck and lance in hand; and as they bore him hither and thither above the cloud with the speed of a charging horse, he was attacking the evil spirits with fierce and mighty thrusts of his lance as if they were mortal men: it seemed he would surely kill them all. The people on the ship stood watching in awe; and the tempest suddenly crashed down on the knight carried by the four demons and on all embroiled in the battle; it struck with such force that it split the mountain in four, and the whole kingdom plummeted into an abyss along with every living being. In moments there was nothing to be seen: it had plunged into Hell with the whole vast horde of demons; and the sky began to shine as bright and fair as a beautiful summer's day. Gadifer and the mariner were filled with awe at this glaring vision of the vengeance of the Sovereign God.

Flamine, realising her mother's prophecy had come true, bewailed her father's dismal fate and railed against sorcery and magic. 'Curse you!' she cried, 'for driving him to such proud heights that he ceased to recognise his Creator! If it hadn't been for you he'd have been the wisest man in the world!'

The Fish-Knights

The author of Perceforest sends his knights out to confront a world of amazing beauty and awesome marvels. The complexity of the created world, and the author's fascination with it, are nowhere expressed as startlingly as in an adventure encountered by 'the White Knight' – King Perceforest's son Betidés – when he's stranded on a distant island.

He searched the isle in vain for any sign of habitation. Then, as he wandered down to the winter sea and came to the shore, he saw the most extraordinary fishes come leaping from the water on to dry land. One of them had a head like an ox with a long horn, and it was all hairy; it had four legs, too, and although they were only two feet long its body and tail were as big as a bull's. There were several fish like horned sheep, all covered in hair except for their fish-like tails. Other fish were like stags and there were many like bears – except they had short legs; and all these fish leapt from the sea and, in the White Knight's presence, started feeding on grass and roots and the leaves of trees, each according to its nature. As soon as they were done they plunged back in the sea, leaving the young knight utterly amazed.

With no sign of life anywhere on the island Betidés had nothing to eat. By the next day he was desperately hungry. Then once again he saw all kinds of fish come leaping from the sea; they were monstrous and terrifying to behold, but ravening hunger so beset him that he drew his sword and attacked the fish and killed several. But as he started to cut them up he saw four fishes advancing on him: they were the size of hunting dogs, though they had only two legs, and on their broad and powerful chests sat heads in the form of helmets tipped with a pointed horn like a sword-blade, three yards long; and on their backs they had a thing like a shield that covered their spine from head to fish-like tail. Betidés watched their bold and purposeful advance with awe; and as they drew near, one of them rose up and dealt him such a blow with its horn that it sent him staggering. Astounded that a fish could hit him so, the knight raised his sword and struck the fish on the head – but to little effect: the fish ducked and the sword fell on the shield on its back, so tough that it did no damage. The fish dealt a second blow that brought the White Knight to his knees, but realising what he was up against the knight now felled the fish and lopped off its legs. A second fish attacked but broke its sword and had to dive back in the sea; the White Knight killed the third with a blow to the head and decapitated the fourth.

Betidés had defeated the fish but his hunger returned; so he lifted the shield on the fish's back and found that the flesh beneath was white as snow. So he cut off a slice along its spine and ate it, and it was so sweet and appetising that he thought he'd never tasted meat so good. Then he sat wondering how he could escape from the isle, beset as it was by fish so brave that they wouldn't stoop to attacking him all together.

Next morning he saw them again in the distance, surging from the sea as they'd done the day before. And among them was a huge band like the fish he'd fought and killed, and they were advancing in good order like a battalion of men-at-arms. With his back to a rock to protect his rear the White Knight prepared to defend himself. Forward they came and rained blows on his shield, but he struck out with such fury to right and left that soon he'd killed a great number. The dead now lay so thick about him that the living couldn't reach him. A second battalion of fish advanced in serried ranks and used their teeth to drag the dead away. He killed many more as they did so, but the rest were fearless and continued the assault. The fish could only spend two hours out of the water, but as soon as one battalion had to return to the sea a new one emerged. The White Knight was dismayed: he realised they were so many that, however brave his defence, he was sure he was going to die.

The final battalion to rise from the water were bigger and mightier than any he'd yet seen. They advanced in impressive order once again; but when they came within a bowshot of the knight, the king of these knights of the sea called a halt and marched on alone towards the other besiegers and uttered an extraordinary cry. They all instantly withdrew and went down to the sea, and the king came up to the White Knight and cried again. The knight saw the crown on this fish's head and knew he was the king, and interpreted the cry as a challenge to single combat. He stepped up to the king and signalled that he needed to drink and then would do battle. The king of the fishes, who had a noble heart, nodded approval and sat down on his tail, and waited while the White Knight drank from the spring.

Then battle began. The king had a long spike of bone, whiter than ivory, which he thrust from his spine at the angle of a unicorn's horn; he also had his sword jutting straight from his helmet, fully two yards long. The spike was a fearsome weapon and pierced shield and mail and plunged into the knight's leg, bringing blood gushing forth. The knight struck back with a mighty blow that drove the king back on his tail, but it landed with a thud as if it had struck a table and did the shield no harm. On the battle raged until both were wounded and losing blood; then the king delivered another thrust with his spike that smashed through the White Knight's shield, but the knight was deft and agile and gave a sudden twist to his shield that snapped the spike in half. Still neither could gain the upper hand and finally, drained, they slumped together on the ground, side by side. The other fish knights were about to surge forward and kill Betidés, but their king uttered another outlandish cry whereupon they all returned to the sea but two.

The king now laid his spike and his sword along his back as a sign of peace, and they rested there together until he could stay out of the water no longer; then he hauled himself up and plunged into a ditch beside the spring. The knight followed him; and as they wallowed and drank, one of the two knights of the sea who'd stayed behind went and fetched from the waves a blood-red fish about the size of a turtle. The king tore it with his teeth and ate some, and was instantly healed of all his wounds; then he gave part of it to Betidés and signalled that he should eat it, too, and the worthy knight, seeing that it had healed the king and was being given to him for the same purpose, decided to do so; and the moment he swallowed it he found himself, to his astonishment, as hale and hearty as ever. Then the king gave him a courteous bow and headed back to the sea. Betidés escorted him to the water's edge, and the king behaved with all the civility and good manners of a human. The Sovereign God is to be praised indeed for His work: He has clearly shown His powers in the qualities with which He has endowed His creatures. And truly, when this fish king came to the sea's edge he turned to the knight and indicated that he should take note of the forces at his command, and Betidés looked out to sea and saw fish knights beyond number, their sword-tipped heads and shielded backs visible above the water, packed in serried ranks for fully half a league. It was an amazing and beautiful sight:

their swords standing tall were like a forest on the sea. They all made way before their king as he swam back into their midst faster than a crossbow bolt, and all his knights swept after him and the vast shoal disappeared.

Next day, however, they all returned at the usual time, and the king came and bowed to Betidés and had one of his fish knights beheaded and offered it to him to eat. The worthy knight declined, but the king and his knights began to feed on the grass, which they loved so much that they wouldn't let anyone live on that isle. And when they'd eaten their fill they divided into two bands and engaged in one of the most awesome tournaments ever seen. And – you might not believe this – the fish king tugged Betidés with his teeth as a sign that he should join in. He did so; and the fish knights learnt so much from his example that he had to strive as hard to show his prowess against them as he had at the tournament at the king of Cornwall's coronation! These knights of the sea preferred to fight with him than with each other, and deemed none worthy of respect until they'd tested themselves against him. The tournament lasted more than an hour; then they took their leave of him and returned to the sea.

The Sleeping Beauty

Perceforest has been described as 'a mine of folkloric motifs', and is famous for featuring this, the first written version of the story that has come to be known as 'the Sleeping Beauty'.

Troylus was riding in search of the beautiful Zellandine, whom he loved more dearly than himself. He rode through a near-deserted land until he found himself by the sea and came upon a ship blown off course by wind and tide. The crew told him they'd been heading for England but were now at the furthest tip of Scotland. They'd been sent from their home country of Zeeland to find a knight named Zelandin, urgently summoned by his father because:

'A great wonder has just occurred in our land. Zellandine, the daughter of our lord Zelland, returned recently from Britain, and two days later the strangest thing happened – it's hardly credible: she was sitting with the other maidens when she fell so deeply asleep that she hasn't woken since! Her father is beside himself with worry.'

It's no wonder that Troylus was distressed by this news: Zellandine was the woman he loved most in all the world. The sailors told him doctors had been powerless to help her, and he begged them to take him across to Zeeland, because 'I know a good deal about medicine thanks to my father – he was one of the finest doctors in the world.'

They set sail at once, and put Troylus ashore on the isle of Zeeland, which is completely flat, having no hills or valleys and very little woodland. That night he took lodging with an elderly lady who told him more about Zellandine's plight:

'She was in her chamber with two of her cousins when she took a distaff laden with flax and began to spin. But she'd barely begun when she lay down, overcome by sleep, and she hasn't woken, drunk or eaten since – though she's lost no weight or colour. Everyone's amazed she's still alive, but they say the goddess Venus, whom she's always served, keeps her in good health.'

Troylus earnestly asked to be shown where she was, for he'd do anything in his power to help, and the lady said she'd gladly direct him to her because 'my son loves her so much that I fear for his life if she dies!'

When Troylus heard he had a rival he was stricken with jealousy. The lady saw his countenance change and guessed the reason; but, clever woman that she was, she gave no sign of this. Instead she led him to a chamber where, I know not by what art, the moment she left he was suddenly quite lost: he had no recollection of Zellandine – he might as well never have seen her; in fact he was like an idiot, with no memory of anything! In his mindless state he suddenly felt the urge to be gone from the room, and he climbed through a window and wandered off into the forest. Next day he was in the open fields, where he lost his shoes in the clinging mud and was soaked to the skin by the pouring rain – but he hadn't the wit to be aware of his plight.

Several days later he staggered into the castle of Zellandine's father, the lord Zelland. As he stood gawping like a half-wit at the pictures that adorned the walls of the hall, a born fool – a simpleton – of Zelland's household looked at Troylus and suddenly said:

'Come and sit down with the others, master: you'll cure the lovely Zellandine!'

And so saying, he tugged with all his might at Troylus's cloak. Troylus pulled away so sharply that the poor fool tumbled to the floor, but as soon as he was up again he was back to his tugging, trying to pull Troylus over to the doctors who were debating what to do to help their lord's sleeping daughter. He finally gave up and came to Zelland and said:

'Forget these doctors, sir! You only need this fool! He's the one who'll cure your daughter!'

'Be off with you, you simple fellow!' said Zelland, who set little store by his words.

'What, Zelland? You don't believe me? I promise you she'll never be cured by anyone but him. He's got the remedy!'

Zelland took no real notice, but rose and came to Troylus and asked him where he was from. Troylus, whose mind had been altered by herbs or spells, replied so inanely that Zelland took him for a simpleton, and turned back to his doctors. But they could tell him nothing – only that what had happened to his daughter wasn't natural, and that he should lock her in a tower to await the will of the gods, whose ways are mysterious.

Zelland was distressed by their lack of a solution but did as they advised. He had the girl carried to the very top of the tower and laid in a bed, as perfectly prepared as could be; he then had every entrance to the tower blocked up except the topmost window, facing east, in the room where his daughter lay. Then he and his sister went to see her once a day to find out if the gods had taken pity on her – but they always found her in the same state, neither better nor worse.

One day after visiting her Zelland decided to go to a nearby temple called the Temple of the Three Goddesses, built long ago by the ladies of the land in honour of the goddess Venus, of Lucina, goddess of childbirth, and of Themis, goddess of destiny, and there he prayed for their mercy on his daughter Zellandine. Now Troylus, for all his distracted state, was fond of Zelland, and had followed him there; and he chanced to fall asleep in a corner of the temple so that Zelland went home without him. And as he slept, about midnight a lady appeared to him and said:

'Arise, knight!'

This lady was of the noblest bearing and wondrous beauty. Her face was very hot and flushed, and her eyes were bright and alluring and seemed on the point of tears – not of grief or anger but of pleasure and excitement. Her head was most elegantly adorned, her shining, almost golden hair arrayed in two tresses; and her garments were green, embroidered with little golden birds. Seeing this glorious lady in his dream, Troylus wondered who she could be and where she was from, for she seemed very forward and had clearly not yet given up worldly pleasures. She evidently wanted some response; he thought the least he could do was bid her welcome, so he stood up with courteous words of greeting and asked her who she was. She laughed out loud and said:

'I am the goddess of love, sir knight! I know how to help and guide all true lovers, and because I know you to be a true lover I shall cast off your affliction.'

So saying, she came up to the knight and raised her hand and moistened her middle finger with saliva, and then dabbed it on his eyes and ears and lips; and in his dream it seemed to him that a veil had been lifted from his sight and his befogged memory was restored to him and he remembered all things past. He peered about as if he'd emerged from darkness into daylight, and saw the goddess – but she was suddenly gone. A moment later he awoke bewildered, the more so at finding himself alone in the temple, lit only by three lamps burning before the three goddesses. Uncertain how he'd come to be there, he made his way to the temple door – but it was locked fast.

He had to bide his time till morning, when an old man came and opened up. When he saw Troylus he recognised him as Zelland's fool and said:

'What are you doing here, fool? Why didn't you go home yesterday with our lord Zelland?'

'Worthy sir,' Troylus replied, 'I may not be as clever as I might be but I'm not a fool!'

The old man apologised for the word but told Troylus he'd seen him behaving like a simpleton ever since he arrived a week before. Troylus was more than a little puzzled, imagining he'd been in the land just a single night; but the old man insisted it was so, and 'I don't know if you remember, but the moment he saw you Zelland's fool said to his master: "Here's the doctor who'll cure your daughter!"'

Troylus, struggling to grasp all this, said: 'Now that you remind me of the girl's affliction, I pray you tell me how it came about.'

'Truly, sir,' the old man said, 'there's not a doctor in the land who can explain it. But I'll tell you what the midwives are saying. They have a custom in this land that, when a woman is a week from her confinement, she comes to the temple with a company of other women to make her devotions to the three goddesses who're worshipped here. Then on the day of the delivery they have one of their chambers splendidly prepared, and a table spread with all manner of food and drink, with three jugs of the finest spiced wine, three goblets and three knives. And when the pregnant woman has given birth to her child, the three attendant goddesses go and eat at the table in secret, invisible to all. Each goddess finds her plate laden with all kinds of delicacies, her jug full and her goblet and her knife laid ready. The goddess Lucina has pride of place since she has brought the creature into the world – dead or alive. Next to her sits the goddess Venus, who has her torch ready to fire the child, as soon as it's born, with that vital heat, filling each limb to the child's capacity – be it male or female – so that he or she can put it to good use at the due and appropriate age. And next to her sits Themis, goddess of destiny, who immediately determines the child's life and all that will befall it – bitter or sweet as the goddess chooses. And what the midwives now fear is that, at the birth of Zellandine, the goddesses were perhaps not welcomed in the manner they would wish, so that all three – or two or one alone – felt aggrieved, and that may be the cause of the girl's affliction.'

'Indeed, dear father,' said Troylus, 'I've heard so much good of the girl that I'm sorry she's so troubled. Please tell me where she is now.'

'She's lying in a strong tower where her father Zelland has had her placed, alone, away from everyone. He's entrusted her to the protection of the gods, for the doctors say medicine's powerless.'

While they were talking Zellandine's aunt – Zelland's sister – arrived at the temple to pray to the three goddesses to have pity on her niece. Troylus, too embarrassed by his wretched state to face her, slipped away and headed into the forest.

As he neared a spring beside a huge oak, he saw a horse tethered to a lance fixed in the ground, and a shield was hanging from the saddle. They were the very lance and shield he'd brought to that land. And lying on the ground was a knight clad in Troylus's own armour. He was astonished – until he remembered the lady who'd given him lodging and had said that a son of hers was in love with Zellandine. Troylus was fired with rage and jealousy, but was so noble hearted that he wouldn't recover his arms by treachery or wheedling but with the edge of a sword – if only he had a weapon; but what was he to do? He hadn't so much as a stick! Then he had an idea: he took the shield from the saddle along with the left stirrup, which would make a good and heavy weapon. Just as he did this the knight stood up, ready to ride to the castle to find news of his beloved Zellandine. The moment he saw Troylus he said:

'Who do you think you are, boy? How dare you take my shield and stirrup?'

'I'm one,' said Troylus, 'who claims this shield and the mail on your back in the name of a knight who left them at a lady's house where he lately took lodging. He left there without them – though he's no idea how – and now I challenge you on his behalf! Take them off or do battle!'

'What?' cried the knight. 'You wretched little nobody! You dare to threaten me? You're not worthy to fight me and not equipped to defend yourself!'

He aimed a mighty blow at him, but Troylus blocked it with his shield and whirled the stirrup three times like a sling and struck the knight on the helm with such force that he was completely stunned. Troylus leapt forward and snatched the sword from his grip, then dealt him a second blow with the stirrup that laid him flat on the ground. He threatened to behead him unless he answered his demands. The knight admitted he was the son of the lady who'd given him lodging, and that she'd used the power of certain herbs to deprive him of his memory and left him to wander witless from her house into the forest. Troylus made him agree to go to Zelland and 'tell him the idiot knight thanks him deeply for the kindness he showed him in his time of need, and say I'm sending you as his prisoner to avenge the wrongs that you and your mother did the knight.' Then Troylus took back his arms and mounted the knight's horse and set off, leaving him to make his way on foot to surrender to Zelland.

As he rode in urgent search of the castle where Zellandine lay sleeping, Troylus found himself once more near the temple to the three goddesses. He decided to go and pray to Venus for guidance, and knelt before her statue and told her:

'That beautiful girl is my life and my death: if she dies I shall despair. All my joy will be lost and I'll die a shameful death – if any death can be shameful when love is the cause.'

He prayed until the sun went down and it was dark inside the temple. And the goddess Venus, who is most merciful and well disposed to lovers who appeal to her for help – and who takes great pleasure in delivering love's ultimate reward – heard his prayers. Suddenly Troylus heard a female voice saying:

> 'Be not troubled, noble knight.
> If you've the valour
> To enter the tower
> Where that noble-hearted beauty
> Lies still as stone,
> When you pluck from the slit
> The fruit that holds the cure,
> The girl will be healed.'

Troylus was overwhelmed: it seemed that if he could do as the verses said, he would cure Zellandine! But he was frustrated that he didn't understand the meaning of the words, and he couldn't help crying aloud:

'Ah, noble goddess! You've brought me such comfort! But when I reach the tower, guide me to the slit and teach me how to pluck the fruit and how to use it to cure the girl!'

No sooner had the worthy Troylus said this than he heard the same voice answer, saying:

> 'The verses have no need of gloss!
> I'll just say this:
> Love will find the slit
> And Venus, who knows the fruit so well,
> Will pluck it:
> Nature will see to that!
> If you're a man, be on your way!
> We don't need all this talking!'

Troylus still felt none the wiser, but he left the temple and set off, pondering on the verses from which he could plumb no meaning. All he knew was that he was determined to find the tower.

With the help of an old woman he at last found the way, but when he reached the castle he saw it was protected by deep moats and a raised drawbridge. And the tower in which Zellandine lay was amazingly high, and every door and window had been filled in with solid stones – all except one at the very top, facing east. Troylus saw a messenger riding towards the castle, who confirmed that the girl lay on that topmost storey and 'only her father Zelland goes there: they say he enters the tower by an underground passage. And because he wants the gods to come and cure her he's placed her in a bed way up there – with a window facing east because he has great faith in the god of the sun.'

Not wanting to be seen, Troylus hid in a thicket of alder trees while he pondered how to find a way into the tower. All day he stayed there, fretting. Finally night fell, and his heart and body burned at the thought of the beautiful Zellandine. Made reckless by love, he rode to the edge of the castle moat and plunged in, and Fortune, who tends to favour the brave, saw him safe to the other side. But the walls were solid, impregnable, impossible to scale, and Troylus slumped to the ground in despair and railed against the god of Love, 'profligate with your promises but the meanest of givers! Were it not for the faith I have in your dear and merciful mother, the goddess Venus, I'd give up on all your promises!'

Just as he said this there was a brief and violent blast of wind, and a moment later he saw a messenger walking straight towards him over the water of the moat. The astonished Troylus asked him who he was looking for, and the messenger replied:

'Troylus of Royalville. Do you know where I might find him?'

'Well, I'm pretty sure he's in this land, but I wouldn't want to say much more – I don't know who his friends and foes are.'

'Truly,' said the messenger, 'if you knew me as well as I know you, you wouldn't hide his whereabouts, for I can help him more than anyone – in fact, he'll never achieve what he wants without me.'

'Who are you, good sir, who can help him so much?'

'I am who I am,' he replied, 'and what I say is true.'

Troylus was unsettled by the messenger's words and feared some trickery. 'I wish you were with him,' he said, 'so he could hear you and see if you're telling the truth.'

'Sir,' said the messenger, 'if I'd thought he was somewhere else I wouldn't have come here! There's no point in hiding: I know you're Troylus! And I know you're trying to find a way into this tower at the prompting of the goddess Venus. If you want to get in you'd better talk to me – what the two of you decide to do then is your business!'

Troylus was as startled by his words as by his crossing of the moat dry-footed. 'Who are you, good sir?' he asked again.

'One,' replied the messenger, 'who can get you into the tower in an instant, in total safety.' Troylus was amazed, but the messenger assured him: 'Just as I crossed the water without wetting my feet, so I'll get you into the tower without a ladder – and down again when it's time.'

Troylus, burning with desire to be with his beloved, agreed to do whatever he said.

'In that case,' said the messenger, 'I'll transport you to where the girl lies in the tower. While you're there, follow the urgings of the goddess Venus and then, once midnight's passed and I call to you, come to me at the window and do as I say.'

And thereupon Troylus felt himself swept into the air, and the next thing he knew he was perched, to his astonishment, on the window ledge a hundred cubits[10] above the ground. He clambered inside the tower and, hardly daring to look for fear it might all be an illusion, peered about the room. And there to one side of the chamber stood a gorgeous bed, worthy of a queen, its curtains and canopy whiter than snow. He was bowled over with excitement: the blood rushed to his cheeks; his whole body was aflame; he was sure it was the bed where the girl lay, ever-sleeping. He couldn't find the courage to approach: like all true lovers, he was bold in thought and a coward in deed! But at last he stepped forward and drew back the curtain and saw, lying there, the one he loved most in all the world. She was stark naked, and his heart and legs gave way and he had to sit down on the edge of the bed. When the Love-ruled knight had recovered a little, he heard the girl breathing so gently in her sleep that it was exquisite to hear, but he could hardly see her in the dim lamplight. But he lit a candle and placed it at the foot of the bed; then he could clearly see her face, as she slept as sweetly as if she'd fallen asleep that moment, so perfect was the colour of her tender cheeks. Troylus was more in love with her than ever; and it seemed that if he called to her there'd be nothing to stop her waking, so he leaned close to her ear and whispered:

'Wake, my love, and speak to me!'

But the girl could neither wake nor speak and gave no response or sign of having heard. He nudged her with his finger several times but she didn't stir at all, and when Troylus saw that nothing he could say or do would wake her he was most distressed. He gazed at the sleeping girl, beautiful as a goddess, soft, rose-red and lily-white. He couldn't help weeping, and wondered aloud:

'Have you been poisoned or enchanted by someone envious of the gifts and graces bestowed upon you by the Sovereign God – or is it the gods' vengeance for some wrong done by your father and your mother?'

While he lamented and gazed at her beauty, Love summoned him to kiss her, and he said: 'Would you like me to kiss you, girl?'

He was about to do that very thing when Reason and Discretion marched forward and said: 'Sir knight, no man should breach a girl's

---

[10]   A cubit was a measurement based on the length of the arm to the elbow – i.e. about half a yard (50cms).

privacy without her leave, and he certainly shouldn't touch her while she sleeps!'

Hearing this he drew back from her face, so close to his; but Desire was beginning to prick him in earnest, and told him her privacy was no reason to desist – Reason had no place in such matters! – and Honour was not in danger because a kiss could cure all manner of ills: it was especially good at reviving from a swoon or calming a troubled heart. Troylus was delighted with this argument and felt Reason couldn't possibly reply; so he kissed the girl more than twenty times. She didn't stir but she did turn redder; she was clearly fast asleep, but he told himself that since she was changing colour, it was a sign she felt something. And seeing her warm flush, she looked so beautiful to him that he couldn't restrain himself: he kissed her countless times and took great pleasure in it – but the pleasure wore off when she didn't respond. Mightily frustrated he said:

'Ah, Venus, goddess of lovers! You promised me that if I found a way inside this tower, Love would point me to the slit that houses the fruit that'll cure the girl! You'll have to show me how to pluck it – I don't know where it grows! Keep your word, noble goddess, for unless the girl recovers, nothing will be more certain than my death!'

Throughout this lamentation he kept gazing at the girl, and he couldn't help kissing her again, she was so beautiful. And while he was accepting these gifts from her lips, the goddess Venus arrived at his side, invisible, and whispered to his heart:

'What a coward you are, knight! You're all alone with this beautiful girl, the one you love above all others, and you don't lie with her!'

He considered these words and decided to act on them. With Venus's flame firing his heart, he felt inspired to throw off his clothes. But Propriety, directed by the god of Love, told him it would be a betrayal to do this: no true lover would harm his beloved. Troylus had second thoughts; and when Venus saw him demur she was more than disappointed with him, and lit her torch and set him so aflame that he was nearly driven wild by the heat. What's more, she made him consider that no faint heart ever won fair lady – and that the girl wouldn't mind what he did, whatever she might pretend! The knight jumped up and was out of his armour and clothes in a second. He dived under the blanket and alongside the girl, who lay there naked, white and soft. Finding himself in this privileged position, Troylus thought no

man had ever been as fortunate as he – if only the girl would speak;
but she didn't yet: the time had not yet come. And although this took
the edge off his joy, he couldn't help answering Venus's urging and
had all he wanted of the beautiful Zellandine – including her right to
the name of maiden. And it all happened while she was asleep: she
didn't stir at all. But then, at the end, she gave a deep sigh, and Troylus
was sure she was about to speak; dumbstruck with alarm he backed
away, ready to act all innocent. As he did so, the one who'd brought
him there appeared at the window and said:

'Come on, sir knight! Keep your promise and do as you're told:
you've done enough for now, and the fruit that'll cure the lovely girl
is plucked!'

Troylus jumped up when he heard the call and threw his clothes
and armour back on, and came to the window where the one who'd
borne him there was waiting. But he was distraught at the thought of
leaving and said: 'Oh, why have you come back so soon? You're taking
me from the deepest bliss in the world!'

'Never mind that! Stay much longer and you'll be in trouble!
Climb on my back and let's go!'

And just as Troylus was clambering on, he heard someone unlock-
ing the chamber door. It was Zelland: while Troylus had been enjoying
himself, the candle he'd lit had shone so bright that Zelland had seen
it from his bed. He'd hurried along the secret passage and, finding
the door to the tower locked, was sure the gods had come to tend his
daughter. So he and his sister had climbed to the chamber and seen
through a crack in the door that the candle had been snuffed out. The
gods, they thought, must have gone, so in they went; and as they entered, Zelland and his sister saw a knight, his arms shining and gleam-
ing in the moonlight, standing on the window ledge, and right outside
was a colossal bird; and they saw the knight climb on to the bird's back
and throw his legs astride its neck; and the bird beat its wings and took
to the air and an instant later had flown from sight. Zelland and his
sister gaped in amazement; then Zelland said it must surely have been
'Mars, the god of battles – we're descended from his line, and he came
to visit my daughter! You saw how majestically he was borne away!'

They hurried to see how Zellandine was and found her sleeping
exactly as before – though her bed was rather rumpled. And Zelland
saw her face was paler than before, and said to his sister:

'The god has given my daughter some medicine to cure her! It's taken away that flush she had! She'll recover now, I'm sure of it – thanks to that god who's kin to us!'

His sister was equally convinced.

Now you need to know that Troylus, distraught at being called from his beloved's side, and leaving only because he'd promised to do as he was told, had hugged and kissed her several times as he took his leave; and as he did so, he found a ring on her finger and took it and slipped it on the little finger of his left hand; and he took another from his own hand – one she'd given him when they first fell in love – and put it in the other ring's place.

When Zelland finally left the chamber he entrusted his daughter to his sister's care. And as she watched a maid putting the bed back in order, she began to wonder whether Mars, the god of battles, might have been rather too familiar with her niece. But she kept these thoughts to herself.

After Zephir carried Troylus from the tower where he'd lain with Zellandine, she remained in bed, exactly as before, for nine whole months without waking, and visited by no one but her aunt, who came to her each day. She had no sustenance but goat's milk which the good lady somehow made her swallow.

And then, one evening at the end of the nine months, fair Zellandine gave birth to a most handsome son. Just after the delivery her aunt came to visit her as usual and found the lovely child beside his mother, who was still fast asleep as ever. The lady was utterly amazed, even more so when she saw the newborn child stretching his neck upward as if seeking his mother's breast, and in doing so finding her little finger and starting to suck upon it eagerly. He kept sucking till he began to cough, and the lady, feeling very sorry for the child, took him in her arms and said:

'Ah, you poor little thing! No wonder you're coughing: there won't have been much milk in there!'

At that very moment the girl awoke and started flailing her arms in bewilderment.

'Zellandine, dear niece!' the lady said. 'How are you? Speak to me!'

And Zellandine, hearing her aunt's voice, replied: 'Dear aunt, I was well enough when I went to bed yesterday, but now I've woken sick! What on earth has happened?'

'It was a little before yesterday!' the lady said. 'For nine months – in which you've shown no sign of waking – you've carried this lovely son in your belly, and today you've given birth to him! But I don't know who his father is.'

When the girl heard this and saw the child she was astounded; but she sensed it was probably true and began to weep, unaware that any man had had dealings with her body. Her aunt tried to comfort her, and explained all that had happened: how she'd fallen asleep and been lodged in the tower by her father so that the gods might visit her, and how she believed that Mars, the god of battles and an ancestor of theirs, had sired the child.

'And in so doing he's restored your health, for which you should give him thanks and praise!'

She was also sure she knew the reason why it had happened: she told Zellandine how she'd prepared the food and drink for the three goddesses on the day of her birth, and how one of them, Themis the goddess of destiny, had taken exception to being without a knife for her food and had decreed that Zellandine's destiny would be such that 'from the first thread of linen that she spins from her distaff a shard will pierce her finger and cast her into a sudden sleep, from which she'll never wake till it's sucked out!' The goddess Venus, her aunt told her, had responded to Themis's ill temper by promising to ensure that it would indeed be sucked from her finger and that all would be made well. And, she said, 'you should take comfort in having given birth to a child sired by such a mighty god as Mars!'

With that, she started rearranging Zellandine's bed. Then suddenly she saw a bird of wondrous shape swoop in through the window: from the breast upward it was in the form of a woman. It landed on the bed where the child lay, took him in its arms, then beat its wings and flew out again, saying: 'Don't worry about the baby!'

The lady and Zellandine watched in horror as the lovely child was swept away. Zellandine was quite distraught, but the lady managed to comfort her; and once she'd recovered, her aunt made the matter known to King Zelland, who was so overjoyed that he held a feast that lasted eight full days, praising the gods who had so splendidly healed his daughter.

Then one day towards the end of April Zellandine was sitting alone at her window, feeling well again in body and spirit and enjoying the clear sky and abundant green. And she looked at her face in a mirror, and was pleased to see that no one would have guessed she'd borne a child. Youth and health were stirring her, and in her growing excitement she remembered Troylus and longed for him. But when she considered her lost maidenhood, she thought his favour would be lost as well: he would be sure to shun her. Then a different thought struck her: what had happened was a complete secret – Troylus would surely never hear of it! As her mind turned this way and that, she looked at the ring that Troylus had given her when she left Britain in exchange for the ring she'd given him. And almost at once she realised that the ring on her finger was the one she'd given Troylus, not the one he'd given her! She was baffled; she didn't know what to think; for surely, if Troylus had tried to come to her while she was asleep, he would never have been able to reach her in the high, strong tower where she'd been locked. She was so bewildered she didn't know what to say or do.

Meanwhile Troylus, who'd been carried back to Britain, couldn't wait to return and find his beloved. At last he found a ship ready to set sail for Zeeland, and after a day and a night he landed and set off at once to find Zellandine. He met six knights resting beside a spring; they were talking excitedly about the beautiful Zellandine, who'd slept for a whole year and now, so people said, had woken through the power and might of the gods; and they told Troylus that, to celebrate her recovery, her father Zelland was holding a great feast at which 'the most valiant knight in the land, hoping to win her love, has summoned all to joust. His name is Nervin.'

Troylus turned hot and cold. He was overjoyed to hear of Zellandine's recovery, but when he heard of Nervin's intentions a shaft of jealousy pierced his heart: such was his torment that a lance could have been thrust through him without shedding a drop of blood – it had turned to ice – and envy made him shake in every limb.

He headed straight for Zelland's castle. After a two-day journey he stopped to rest beneath a hazel tree. And as he lay there something strange happened to him: although he wasn't sleeping he entered an altered state in which he felt he was asleep, and thought he saw far off a beautiful maiden approaching him, bathed in light, who said:

'Rise, sir knight, and come to my lady's house: a knight shouldn't be sleeping in the open.'

And it seemed to him that she took him by the hand and led him to a rushing river fearful to behold, and he pulled back, sure she was about to push him in.

'Are you afraid?' she said. 'I'll go first.'

'Please do!' said Troylus; and the maiden stepped on to the storming water and Troylus followed her, bewildered, thinking he must be dreaming. She led him to the further bank and to a splendid house, and into a magnificent hall with a roaring fire. To one side sat a middle-aged lady dressed in white, who rose to meet him with a smile. Seeing her cheerful welcome he bowed to her, and the lady bade him sit beside the fire and tell her about himself. He told her enough to satisfy her without revealing who he was. Then a maiden came and asked the lady if she should bring her child to the fire, and the lady said she should; thereupon two nurses came carrying a handsome male child which the lady took and cradled in her arms and kissed as she said:

'Blessed young child, from you will spring a noble line leading at last to the most illustrious man in all the world, who'll bring glory to all Britain.'[11]

Troylus was startled by her words and said: 'Is this child your son, my lady?'

'Oh sir,' she replied, 'Fortune hasn't granted me such honour! But he was born of such a noble father and gracious mother and under such favourable stars that I feel fortunate indeed to be his nurse and guardian.'

The noble Troylus gazed at the child and noticed a mark on his right shoulder, the scar still fresh: it was in the shape of a king sitting on a throne holding a naked sword between his teeth and a pair of scales in his right hand. Troylus asked the lady the significance of the mark, and she explained:

'No lady of worth in this land bears a child without marking him with a sign to avoid the trickery of wicked women who bring ill-

---

[1]   The child later proves to be Benuic, who is to be an ancestor of Lancelot of the Lake. This is one of many instances where *Perceforest* introduces the ancestors of the major figures in the Arthurian world.

favoured children into the world: when they find they've produced a bad fruit they often cunningly swap it for a good one!'

'It's a fine custom indeed, lady!' said Troylus. 'And this child is a delight to behold.' And he kissed the boy, who began to laugh. Then they sat down to a generous supper, after which Troylus retired to sleep in a chamber. But next morning, to his astonishment, he awoke beneath the hazel tree.

Fired with thoughts of his beloved Zellandine he rode all day till evening, when he came upon the Temple of the Three Goddesses. He went inside and made his prayers to them, whereupon he heard a voice say:

'We've received your prayers most favourably, sir, as will be seen in your son.'

'Oh, illustrious goddesses,' he said, not realising he had one, 'please tell me how a son will come to me!'

'From you,' the voice replied, 'has come the seed from which will be born the flower of prowess. Ask no more; we're watching over him. Go and complete your mission.'

Commending himself to the goddesses' keeping, Troylus mounted and rode on to Zelland's castle, where he found the jousting had already begun. Zellandine was there in the stands, distressed that her beloved Troylus was missing, while Nervin was performing mighty feats and earning all the acclaim. But now Troylus arrived and unhorsed four knights one after the other, and to Zellandine's joy all attention turned to this new knight. Nervin, enraged, levelled his lance and charged at Troylus, and Troylus met him with a blow that sent him tumbling over his horse's rump. But Zellandine's father wanted to give his daughter to Nervin and made every excuse for him, saying that even the most valiant of knights would sometimes be unhorsed in a joust.

Meanwhile Troylus continued to defeat all comers. Soon he was the last knight left, and at the banquet that night he was honoured with a place at the head of the table, right next to Zellandine. But on the other side sat Nervin, for Zelland still intended to give his daughter's hand to him, and Zellandine was so downcast that she didn't even see Troylus, right there at her side. But Troylus couldn't speak to her with Zelland and Nervin so close.

Then Zelland asked him where he was from, and he replied: 'From Royalville in Scotland.' At this Zellandine's blood stirred from head to toe and she instantly thought of Troylus, whom she hadn't seen for so long. She didn't dare look the knight in the face, but she glanced at his right hand and saw that on his middle finger sat a gold ring mounted with an emerald. She recognised it at once and didn't know what to think: it was the ring exchanged for hers while she'd slept in the mighty tower.

As the banquet ended her father took her aside and told her he'd decided to marry her to Nervin; she asked him to let her consider this till the next day. He agreed, and she sent a maid with a secret message to the knight who'd said he was from Scotland, begging him to take her with him back to Britain. Troylus hurried with the maid to Zellandine's chamber, where she instantly recognised her love; and he told her all that had happened – how he'd lain with her and swapped their rings, been carried back to Scotland and then returned to Zeeland and seen a vision of the beautiful boy from whom the lady guardian had prophesied would come 'the glory of Britain'. Still Zellandine looked downcast, and Troylus asked why.

'Alas,' she said, 'how can I be otherwise when you're the man I love most in all the world, yet my father wants me to marry Nervin? Tomorrow I must agree to be his wife!'

Troylus swept her into his arms and promised to take her back to Britain and marry her. They swiftly had three horses saddled, and mounted in secret and prepared to ride. And as they were about to leave, Zellandine called to her maid:

'Tell my father and my aunt that Mars the god of battles is taking me away to his land because they mean to marry me against my will!'

And with that they departed and rode with all speed to the sea.

The Marvellous Child

One of the most striking characters in the later books of Perceforest is Passelion, son of Estonné and Priande, destined to be an ancestor of no less a figure than Merlin. The following passage tells of his remarkable birth.

The good lady Priande's labour lasted a day and a night and the next day till well past noon. The ladies attending her felt great pity for the trial she was suffering; but her fruit took a break from his struggling and she was able to rest and sleep. And as she slept she dreamt she was with her husband in the middle of a forest, and there the pains of childbirth began. And when her husband saw this he dismounted and started to build a bower around her to hide her secret business a little. Then he withdrew and sat beside a spring. And according to her dream, in the middle of her labour she looked through the leafy branches of her shelter and saw an armed knight emerge from the depths of the forest and thrust a lance clean through her husband's body; he fell dead, and she heard the traitor cry: 'Go straight to Hell, and tell the devils that Bruiant slew you!'

She awoke, crying in horror and agony: 'Seize the treacherous Bruiant who's killed my husband!' The women attending her came running in alarm, and pinned her down for fear the terrible commotion might endanger the child's life; but still she uttered loud and bitter cries of 'Kill the wicked, murderous Bruiant who's slain my husband!' And there followed an extraordinary wonder: the child, nourished to great strength in her belly, was so upset by his mother's cries that the ladies present later recalled hearing him, still in her womb and yearning to be out, utter two shouts not of pain but of fury at the long delay.

Priande passed out and the ladies were afraid she was dead; for a moment they wept in anguish; but then she revived and told Lyriope of her dream and said she was convinced it was true. 'And the child in my belly is enraged that he's not come into the world, such is his desire to avenge his father's death! I know for sure I'm never going to see my son, so I pray you, when he's born, tell him this from me:

"Passelion, do not forget to avenge your father's death".' Then she howled with agony once more, the pain of labour intensified by the vision of her husband's murder; and such was the child's passion to be out of the womb that the natural passage would not suffice: he burst from his mother's right side; the soul instantly left her body, and the child tumbled out and gave a mighty stretch to greet his freedom.

The good lady Lyriope beheld this wonder and was horrified, not without cause; but she took the child and freed him from the shirt in which nature had wrapped him. And she saw that he was an awesome and astounding sight: for in his right hand he clutched a crossbow and in his left a foot-long bolt, both perfectly formed from fleshly sinew. As soon as they were cool and dry both bow and bolt turned hard and strong. The ladies were so astonished that their grieving was forgotten, and Lyriope said to the child:

'Passelion, your mother bids you never forget to avenge your father's death.'

So saying, she tried to take the crossbow and bolt from his hands, but he was gripping them so tightly that she had to let them go.

Night was falling; they lit candles and prepared Priande for burial. And then another amazing thing happened: they suddenly saw – despite the fact that the door was closed – a man standing in the chamber, coarsely, roughly dressed and wearing a hat that entirely hid his face. They were too startled to utter a sound; they sat on the bed where the body lay and watched in silence as the man uncovered the child's feet and started tugging at the toes of his left foot; the child was none too pleased by this and raised his foot and gave him an angry kick on the hand with all the childlike strength he could summon. The man was delighted by this and said: 'You are Estonné's son! Your mother did well to name you Passelion, for you surpass the lion in ferocity and courage!'

And so saying, he vanished from the room so suddenly that they didn't know what had become of him.

As they recovered from their bewilderment, they all agreed that the child was destined for greatness: they all believed it was the god of battles who had come to visit him and endow him with special power.

Priande's dream that her husband Estonné would be murdered comes horribly true: he is treacherously killed by an arch-enemy of Perceforest's knights, a member of Darnant's 'evil clan' named Bruiant the Faithless. The child Passelion, even though not yet two years old, joins the knights who are besieging Bruiant in his castle, bent upon taking revenge.

And Bruiant, peering from a window, heard his enemies saying:

'Welcome, Passelion! Now you can help avenge the death of your father, treacherously murdered by the wicked Bruiant!'

The moment the child heard these words he raised his fist, his face set in the fiercest glare, and Bruiant saw this and was aghast: he'd never seen such an awesome child. And hearing him called Passelion made him more fearful still, for Mars the god of battles had declared that a child of that name would put him to death. If only he could get out of the castle with his life, he thought, he'd go so far that they wouldn't find him in a year.

And so it was that Passelion joined the companions in the siege. It continued uneventfully for ten months.

Then he began to walk; he needed to hold on to his nurse's finger, but he was bigger, stronger and more advanced than any two-year-old. In fact he understood most of what was said to him, especially anything relating to war and combat – and, above all, to the destruction of the wicked Bruiant. Then to everyone's amazement he began to speak, and it occurred to Le Tor that Zephir might have something to do with it. 'After all, he said he would never fail the child, and visited him nightly to rub him all over with herbs, and prophesied he'd be the ancestor of the wisest man of his age.'[12]

Then, that very night as they ate together, young Gadifer, who was impervious to enchantment, saw something appear in the distance and laid his sword ready at his side. Lyonnel asked him what was wrong and he answered:

'Look towards the forest, sir.'

The others could see nothing; but Passelion, in the middle of them all, turned his head that way and instantly called out, saying: 'Damsel, give me that pretty thing!'

The knights were baffled, for seven of them could see no living soul; they gripped their swords, fearing trickery.

---

[12]   Passelion is to be the ancestor of Merlin.

'Sirs,' said Gadifer, 'don't stir from your seats; you'll soon see what is veiled to you now.'

And a moment later they suddenly saw, right in their midst, a maiden most nobly dressed, holding in her hand a rich casket. As soon as she appeared she greeted all the company, but especially Passelion, for she said: 'Passelion, mighty child, this casket is sent to you.'

Then she vanished so suddenly that no one knew what had become of her – except the valiant Gadifer, who saw her mount a palfrey and ride swiftly away.

Passelion was delighted with the casket and immediately started clawing at the lock to open it; and when he found he couldn't he was very cross and cried out in his childish way: 'Let me in here!'

Troylus saw there was a key, and opened it. Inside lay a sealed letter, and Passelion, sitting in Troylus's lap, took it out and said: 'Here you are, uncle.' And Troylus broke the seal and began to read.

Written by 'Morgane the fairy, special friend of Zephir, and nurse and guardian of the noble Benuic, son of the worthy Troylus of Royalville,' it appealed on Benuic's behalf, saying: 'I, Benuic, ask my dear cousin Passelion to receive this gift and follow what is ordained. The influence of Mars came to the fore on the day you burst from your late mother's side to come into this world, and that god's nature is so cruel that most children born at that time die along with their mothers. Being born then as you were, you are destined to be endowed with might, prowess, courage and a generous heart; and that being so, it is the will of the wise Zephir that tomorrow at noon, when Mars's power will be at its zenith, you receive the order of chivalry, and from that hour you shall be the god Mars's marshal in the spilling of blood. And so that you lack nothing necessary for the ceremony, I send it all to you here in this casket.' The letter closed with greetings to 'my dearest father', and Troylus, reading this, was overjoyed as well as astonished, for he had no idea what had become of his son after he'd been carried away by the strange bird from Zellandine in the tower – though he sensed now that the lady and child he'd seen in his strange adventure in the forest must surely have been Morgane and his son.

Inside the casket were all the garments and arms the child needed – all made to fit his little frame – including a hauberk of silver and a helmet and spurs of fine gold, a sword just a foot and a half long, and a gold shield blazoned with an armed and mounted knight and a blue lion, its right arm holding a sword aloft and its left paw resting on its head.

Next day the eight companions prepared the child to be knighted, each arming him according to instructions in the casket. But when Lyonnel gave him the accolade, Passelion was annoyed by the blow on his shoulder and drew his sword and struck Lyonnel on the knee, saying: 'How dare you hit me?!' He drew blood, but the wound wasn't deep and Lyonnel started laughing; but Troylus was angry and shook the child, telling him it was very wrong to strike the knight who'd dubbed him, whereupon Passelion struck his uncle, too, drawing blood from his foot. Gadifer, presenting him with his shield, made the mistake of hitting it with a stick, saying 'Passelion, learn to suffer: there's much to endure in deeds of arms', and promptly found blood running from a wound in his arm; Nestor gave him a blow on the helm and the child swung his sword and drew blood from his leg. The eight lords were amazed and delighted by the fierce might of their young knight, who in the course of nature shouldn't yet have been walking or talking; but laugh though they might, he let all of them feel the edge of his sword: if he'd been of man's age, none would have been his better.

One with no cause to laugh at all was Bruiant: as he watched from his castle he realised the prophecies of Mars and Venus – that he would die at the hand of Estonné's son, and within that year of which there were only three months left – threatened to come true, for he could see the child's growing strength and ferocity and, worse still, saw him now being knighted. He decided to defy the predictions by putting his life at no risk at all: he would stay inside the castle till the year was out.

Once he was knighted, Passelion wouldn't sleep in a cradle with his nurses – he slept alone; and when he felt hungry he knew exactly how to call for them: and though there were three, they were hard pressed to provide him with milk enough to meet his appetite.

Little happened till the last day but one before the end of the year the goddess Venus had predicted would see Bruiant's death. Then the foul murderer grew in pride and confidence, feeling sure he was going to prove the prophecies wrong. As soon as Passelion rose that morning he insisted the knights should arm him, for he'd had news during the night.

'What news?' asked his uncle Troylus.

'I'm not telling anyone till my helmet's on!'

Troylus and the others laughed at this, and Lyonnel said: 'What difference will your helmet make?'

'I may be little,' the child replied, 'but have no doubt: before to-night, before sundown, I shall accomplish what you've not managed, and fulfil what I must do.'

The eight companions were amazed by his words, and Troylus said: 'Dear nephew, who's taught you to say all this?'

'I'll tell you, uncle,' the boy replied, 'when you've armed me, for I can see my mortal enemy at that window, mocking me.' And as soon as he was armed, Passelion vowed: 'I'll be lord of the traitor's castle before morning! And thus I'll avenge his insult to the god Mars, as well as my father's death!' And when Troylus asked how he came to understand his mission, the child replied: 'The good man in the cape told me: every night he tells me what to do next day.' And he told his uncle to be alert that night, for 'you'll witness wonders just before the ascendancy of Mars the god of battles draws to a close.'

Bruiant, watching from a turret, poured scorn, saying: 'Who are you trying to scare with that champion you've armed? Guard the gate as much as you like – I'll be out of here sooner than you think!'

Troylus replied: 'You're like the swan, singing when he's about to die!'

But Bruiant called back: 'Do your worst! I don't fear you or any man alive!'

Passelion, with an awesome countenance, went to find the cross-bow and bolt he'd brought with him from his mother's womb – which is hard to believe, but indeed, many children are born in re-markable ways – and took them to Troylus and said: 'Dear uncle, teach me how to draw this bow.' And when Troylus expressed surprise, Pas-selion said: 'If I'm endowed with sense and understanding before the natural time, and another man stays an idiot all his life, it's all in the gift and power of the Sovereign God. So I want you to show me how to use and shoot this bow, for I feel a natural aptitude.'

The eight companions felt no inclination to laugh at this; they sensed a great authority in the child's words. So Troylus and all the others taught him all they knew of the art of the crossbow; and in no time the boy, born under the influence of Mars and the watchful

eye of Zephir, was shooting with such accuracy that all those who
beheld him were amazed. Then he told them to keep close watch that
night, for 'the constellations are in our favour. So be alert: I'm going
to take milk and then sleep.' And so he did, while the eight companions armed, unsure what was about to happen.

They kept watch till midnight; then a terrible storm arose, and
almost at once it was upon them, sweeping round the castle with
such force that it seemed the walls and towers would crumble into
an abyss. It grew ever stronger, as if all the devils of Hell were inside Bruiant's castle and the marshes round about, and suddenly they
heard a deafening crash at the gate, as if it had collapsed. At that moment Passelion's three nurses came rushing to the companions and
frantically reported that 'the man in the black cape came and took
Passelion, but we don't know where!'

They leapt up and searched high and low through the howling
gale; and Troylus, finding himself before the castle gate, was thrilled
to see that the storm had forced the drawbridge down and battered
down the doors. He was joined there by Le Tor and Lyonnel and then
by their companions; and as they stood in the darkness they heard
Bruiant shouting orders to his eight knights:

'Guard the gate against the besiegers till the storm is over! Demons
have brought the boy Passelion in here! As long as the gate is guarded
I'm not afraid: he's not a man to fear!'

Lyonnel and the others instantly guessed that Zephir had summoned up the storm and carried the boy into the castle. So violent
was the storm that they could hear very little and see next to nothing;
but as they stood in the gateway expecting attack at any moment, they
saw a light appear in the middle of the courtyard and in it they beheld
an enormous horse, and upon it Passelion, armed, sword in hand and
crossbow slung at his side. And as he looked up at a tower that stood
at the castle's heart, the child saw Bruiant at a window and shouted:

'Traitor! Evil murderer! Come down and do battle with me: I
charge you with the treacherous murder of my father!'

Bruiant cried back: 'I'll do no such thing, my good sir! There
wouldn't be much honour in fighting such feeble opposition! Wait
till you've come of age and then ask me again!'

Passelion, enraged, cried: 'It would be a disaster if you lived that
long! Defend yourself as you please: I'm going to kill you this day!'

'That's as much of a lie,' said Bruiant, 'as Venus's prophecy!'

And so saying, he disappeared from the window and climbed to the very top of the tower. Lyonnel and his companions wanted to go after him, but could hardly stand up in the storming wind. But suddenly it abated and day began to break, and in the rays of the sun they saw Passelion sitting on his horse across the entrance to the tower, proud and fierce as an enraged lion; and they saw also that every door and window in the castle had been smashed to the ground by the tempest's force. They heard a commotion in the gatehouse overhead: Bruiant's eight knights were preparing to defend themselves; but with every door off its hinges they could do nothing to stop Lyonnel and his companions running up to attack them, and they slaughtered them all and flung their bodies through the windows into the courtyard, in full view of the wicked traitor who was utterly dismayed – though Passelion was delighted to see the massacre. Then they came down and gave Passelion a joyful greeting, and asked him who had brought him there.

'The man in the cape, sirs,' he replied. 'My father's death upsets him more than anything – as it does me: I desire vengeance more than anything in the world! So I pray you, climb this tower and bring me the foul traitor back alive: I want to deal him the first blow!'

When Bruiant heard them coming up, unhindered by any door, he was terrified, not without cause, and clambered through a window that opened on to the roof. He used a ladder to climb to the roof's very tip, and then flung the ladder into the moat below so that no one could follow him. The companions couldn't find him anywhere, and thought he must have leapt from a window. But his body was nowhere to be seen, and Passelion was convinced he couldn't have left the tower 'or the man in the cape will have lied to me!' At that moment he looked up and saw Bruiant on the pommel of the tower's roof, and called to the knights: 'Sirs, I see Bruiant on the tower's tip!'

And they all looked up and exulted when they saw the child was right. But there was no way of reaching Bruiant, and no way he could get down alive; and Passelion said:

'I must put him to death before nightfall, sirs, or the goddess Venus will appear a liar and Mars the god of battles deceived: he's hastened my growth in mind and body for this very purpose.' And he cried aloud to Bruiant: 'Wicked traitor, what made you go up there? You'd be better dying down here in combat than up on the roof by starving!'

'Truly, Passelion,' Bruiant cried, 'I haven't come up here to die, but to escape the false prophecy of Venus who swore I'd die this year! If I live till tonight she'll be proved a liar. And up here I've nothing to fear from you today – or tomorrow for that matter! Let the gods do their worst – and you, too, their executioner! You're of no account to me, even though I killed your father – and if I had to do it again, I wouldn't rest till I'd killed him with my own hands!'

Passelion was wild with rage and cried: 'Treacherous wretch! You brag of my father's death and insult our mighty gods in my presence! Come down and fight, for that power celestial summons me to do now what it demands of me!'

'Go and have some milk, little boy, and wait till you've grown! And don't believe what the gods tell you: I'll prove them liars!'

Passelion was more incensed than ever by the tyrant's manner. He took the crossbow and gave it to his uncle to load; then he aimed at Bruiant, sitting on the tower's tip, and said:

'The god Mars in heaven wants to see your blood spill, and the goddess Venus prays for vengeance upon you for the monstrous murders you've committed and your violations of so many ladies. For my own part, I madly crave your heart to avenge your crimes – above all the murder of my father.'

And he loosed the bolt and struck Bruiant through the centre of his heart with such force that the point came bursting out behind. Bruiant fell from the tower's tip and rolled down the roof, and the valiant knights, exultant, leapt forward with their naked swords and, before the body hit the ground, sliced it into pieces. When Passelion saw the corpse lying in bits he jumped from his horse, afire with rage, and came to the piece that contained the heart and ripped it apart with his teeth and hands as dogs tear their quarry at the kill. Only when he'd had his fill of ripping his teeth through the evil Bruiant's heart did he begin to calm. Then he stood up and said to the eight princes, all astounded by his ferocity:

'It seems, sirs, that the quest for revenge for my father is now complete, and for your aid in that I thank you all.'

The Death of Caesar

The author of Perceforest draws material from many sources, linking his prehistory of Arthurian Britain to numerous existing traditions and histories. In the following episode, he makes the murder of Julius Caesar an act of revenge for his destruction of Britain. Caesar has led an invasion in which the Romans have annihilated Perceforest's forces in an epic battle and devastated the whole kingdom. The young knight Ourseau, although raised as a Roman, has discovered he's the grandson of King Gadifer of Scotland and his wife the Fairy Queen, and that his father's brother was killed in the battle by Caesar himself. The Fairy Queen wants Ourseau to avenge his uncle's death with the head of Caesar's lance which dealt the mortal wound. She has recovered it from his uncle's body, and given it to Ourseau to carry back to Rome, where his father greets him with the utmost joy.

But he had grave news: 'Dear son, you've lost your mother and your dear grandfather – and two of your brothers also: they were killed in a battle fought by the senators against Julius Caesar who's lately returned from Gaul.'

'Truly, honoured father,' said Ourseau, 'it's not the first harm Caesar's inflicted on those close to us.' And he told his father how, as he had bidden him, he'd gone to Britain to learn the truth about their ancestry, and found that Caesar had devastated the land. 'I travelled for more than six months without finding a city, town or house left standing, and the few people who survived were wilder than any deer or fox, living in the forests like beasts.' But at last he'd found some of his ancestors, and he told his father the whole story of their descent from the king and queen of Scotland.

His father was overcome with joy, as were his brothers when they heard the news. But Ourseau stressed that their great forefather Gadifer and his brother Perceforest and the knights of Britain 'would have been the mightiest in all the world if Julius Caesar hadn't destroyed them and their land through the treachery of Luces and Cerse.' He told them of the Roman girl Cerse's disastrous marriage to Perceforest's son Betidés, and how Caesar had taken advantage of her treachery to invade Britain unopposed before destroying the outnumbered Britons at the Franc Palais: there was no honour, he said, in Caesar's victory.

And there was more to tell: he had also seen the hideously muti-
lated bodies of two of his father's brothers, Gadifer and Nestor, 'their
wounds still as red as the day of the battle'; and the Fairy Queen had
given him the head of Julius Caesar's lance, recovered from Nestor's
body, with which she'd prophesied Caesar himself would die; and
'she asked me to give it to her son – our father, sitting here before me
– and to tell him to have pity on his slaughtered kin.' And in conclu-
sion Ourseau told how his wife had stolen the lance-head to try to
stop him going to Rome, and how the spirit Zephir had helped him
recover it from a smith who had turned it into twelve needles.[13] And
Zephir, he said, had told him to guard them well, for 'only with these
needles will Julius Caesar be put to death'; he had prophesied, too,
that there would be only one day and one night when Fortune would
desert Caesar and allow him to be killed, a day when all the doors and
windows of his house would create a clattering din[14] and alarm the
whole of Rome.

Knowing now that Caesar had 'killed the king my uncle and two of
my brothers as well as two of my sons', Ourseau's father told his sons
that 'if I were as young as you I'd risk my life to put him to death!'

[13]   We are earlier told that the lance-head has been turned into twelve objects like 'needles
[aguilles] for sewing silk'. But the word used here is 'greffes' and should probably be translated more exactly as 'styluses'. The idea that Caesar was killed with writing-styluses ultimately comes from Suetonius's description of the murder. In line with all other classical
accounts, Suetonius says that Caesar was attacked by his assassins with daggers – 'pugioni-
bus'; but he uniquely refers to Caesar retaliating by using his writing-stylus – his graphium
– to stab Casca in the arm: 'Caesar Cascae brachium arreptum graphio traiecit' ('Caesar grabbed
Casca's arm and ran it through with his stylus'). Suetonius, Lives of the Twelve Caesars, Book
I, Chapter 82. But the Perceforest author will almost certainly have been following, rather
than the Latin original, the French translation of Suetonius in the highly influential Li
Fet des Romains (c.1215), where he would have read that 'Cassius le feri de son grefe en la gorge…
Suetoines dist que Cesar esracha a un senator son greffe de la main; Casce estoit apelez, et l'en feri parmi le braz.
Lors s'esforça Cesar de saillir fors; mes ne pot, car Brutus le feri dou sien grefe el piz.' Li Fet des Romains, ed.
Flutre & Vogel (Paris, 1937), p.740.
[14]   This detail, too, is probably derived ultimately from Suetonius, in which 'the very night
before his murder… his wife Calpurnia thought the pediment of their house had fallen,
and that her husband was stabbed in her arms; and suddenly the doors of their chamber
flew open by themselves'. Suetonius, Lives of the Twelve Caesars, Book I, Chapter 81). The
likelihood is, however, that the author will again have been following the translation of
Suetonius in Li Fet des Romains; there, almost identically, he would have read: 'Cele nuit meisme
fu il vis a sa fame Calpurnia que li combles de sa meson chaoit et li ocioit son mari en son devant; et lues avint
soudainement que totes les fenestres de la sale et li huis de la chambre ou il gisoit ovrirent ensanble de lor gré a un
froïs.' Li Fet des Romains, ed. Flutre & Vogel, p.739.

One of the brothers, Ursus Bellicus, was hot-headed and proposed an immediate march to Caesar's palace where they would 'kill him and then save ourselves as best we can!' But another, Ursus Bouchesuave,[15] said they needed to be shrewder, saying: 'There's no revenge in killing your enemy and then being killed yourself!' They should bear in mind Zephir's prophecy that 'Fortune would withdraw her hand from Caesar for just one night and day' and wait for the promised omen to appear. Meanwhile, he said, the twelve needles should be kept in a safe and secret place, for Caesar must be killed, as bidden by the Fairy Queen, with the lance-head he'd used to slay their uncle Nestor. This they all agreed.

And Fortune for the moment was indeed on Caesar's side: after conquering the whole of Gaul he heard that Britain had a new king, Cassibellanus, who was failing to pay due tribute to Rome, so he invaded once more; and though he was driven back ignominiously by Cassibellanus and his valiant knights, Cassibellanus was in conflict with Endroger, duke of Trinovantum – now called London – and this rebel allied with Caesar and together they crushed Cassibellanus. And when Caesar returned to Rome he steadily rose in power, eliminating Pompey and Cato and finally being made emperor.

By this time Ourseau's father was dead, but Ourseau and Ursus Bouchesuave and several of their brothers remained alive; and Ursus had a son, also named Ursus Bouchesuave for his wisdom and eloquence, who was even more respected in the Senate than his father had been: his opinion in all matters was valued above all others. And he reminded Ourseau and his brothers that, though Fortune had now set Caesar at the highest point She could, 'Fortune is fickle, and Julius will find that the higher a man rises, the more painful will be his fall. There are few worthy men in Rome who, thanks to Caesar, haven't lost a father or a brother or uncles or cousins, and they hate him for it.' All they had to do, he said, was wait for the omen prophesied by Zephir.

And then one night it happened. They heard a terrible noise coming from the emperor's palace, as if a violent storm was about to bring it crumbling down; and a squire brought word that: 'The doors and windows are slamming back and forth against the walls – half of them are lying in the street!'

---

[5]   This might be translated as 'Sweet-tongue'.

Ursus Bouchesuave rode to Caesar's palace and found a great crowd gathered there, including many of the consuls. Among them were Cassius and Brutus; they spoke secretly with Ursus, and Brutus said he was sure the sign was 'an ill omen for the emperor! I can't believe his rapid rise will go unpunished – he's won his high station and the honour he enjoys by slaughtering two hundred thousand men and destroying the city's liberties!' And, certain that Caesar had killed his father, Brutus declared: 'I'd exult if he met with an accident! I'd strike the first blow to murder him – he's reigned too long!'

Ursus, overjoyed to hear this, seized the opportunity and told them of Zephir's prophecy to Ourseau.

Cassius and Brutus didn't hesitate. 'We're your kinsmen on your mother's side,' they said, and they promised to join the brothers in the plot and each would take one of the twelve needles. With vows of utter secrecy they parted.

Next morning the senators all gathered at the Capitol. When Caesar arrived to join them he told them what had happened the night before, and asked them to 'commission your finest astronomers to discover the meaning of it all.' But Ursus replied: 'Julius Caesar, our lord and emperor, there's no need to summon astronomers or any other learned men to explain the signs. They were prophesied and predicted after you destroyed Britain and the noble King Perceforest, from whom I'm directly descended! They signified that the god of Fortune has withdrawn from you his hand of blessing, at the request of the gods of Rome who protest and grieve at the loss of the city's liberties. The public weal, the honour and the freedom of the citizens you have stolen and usurped with your tyrannical power. But now Fortune, ever fickle, ever blind, realising Her mistake, has left you, as all the people heard from the noise she made last night as she departed![16] And we who sit as judges and guardians of the honour and common weal of the city have considered this matter and reached a decision which I, at my colleagues' bidding, will pronounce.' And Ursus turned to the senators and said: 'Sirs, according to Roman custom take up your styluses and write your judgement on your tablets.'

And he stood up and presented to the twelve most eminent senators the twelve needles that Ourseau had brought from Britain. Julius

---

[16]   i.e. with the clattering doors and windows.

Caesar, who was emperor of Rome and lord of all the world and had the obedience of all men in the world but twelve, was disconcerted now, standing bare-headed and speechless before them. In their presence he had lost all princely bearing except for a clenched right fist. Then Ursus, seeing it was time to act and that delay could be fatal, spoke up, saying:

'Considering the case of Julius, here before us, who has worked against the common weal and the honour and liberty of the city of Rome and against the lives of the noble men of our land – he is responsible for the deaths of a father or brother or beloved kinsman of every one of us here – I sentence him for this cruelty to die by the twelve needles we hold. They shall strike him till his soul is parted from his body, and thus the prophecy of the Fairy Queen and the wise Zephir will be fulfilled, and vengeance taken for the deaths at his hand or his command of the noble men of Britain and all those dear to us.' Then Ursus turned to his companions and said: 'Follow me, sirs.'

And they replied: 'We shall follow.'

Then Ursus Bouchesuave rose to his feet and said: 'I, foremost among you, shall strike the first blow.'

And then something amazing happened: Pity suddenly left that chamber and the heart of every man within it. Ursus Bouchesuave walked forward while the noble emperor Julius stood like a statue, motionless and speechless;[17] and Ursus plunged the full twelve inches of the needle into his chest. All the others followed suit, until the valiant emperor fell dead upon the floor; but because of the tiny punctures made, he shed not a single drop of blood.

When the deed was done the accomplices and all those present were appalled and repented in their hearts; but Ursus, the strongest and the wisest of them, said: 'It's pointless being dismayed now, sirs! What's done cannot be undone. Take heart, and let's bring this to an honourable and favourable close.'

Stirred to lion-hearted courage they replied: 'Well said – but what should we do now?'

'I'll tell you,' he said. 'First, to hide our guilt we'll take advantage

---

[7]   According to Suetonius, Caesar 'was stabbed twenty-three times, but uttered not a word, only a groan at the first blow'. Suetonius, op.cit., Chapter 82. *Li Fet des Romains* (op. cit., pp.740-1) translates this exactly as '*reçut .xxiii. plaies sans mot soner, ne mes que il gemit un petit a la premiere plaie*'.

of the absence of any blood or mark of violence upon his body. Open the doors of the Capitol, and call in the princes and knights who're waiting outside for the emperor; we'll tell them he suddenly fell dead here before us, just after he'd asked the meaning of those signs last night – the harbingers of his death.'

'Good advice indeed!' they all replied.

'It's strange,' said Ursus, 'that Julius, always so valiant, wise and bold, made no reply to the charges I levelled against him, and no attempt to defend himself – he just stood there with his right hand clenched. Let's see if he's holding something before we announce his death.'

He stepped forward and took hold of Julius's right hand. It was rigid – in giving up his soul he'd clenched his fist so tightly that it had to be prised open. Inside it Ursus found a letter, fastened with a seal that couldn't be identified, as the wax had been crushed by the clenching of his fist. Ursus could hardly wait to see the contents; and when he opened it he read the following words:

'Noble emperor, do not go to the Capitol this day, for your death awaits you there. Tomorrow you may do as you wish.'

Ursus read it aloud for all his companions to hear, and he remembered Zephir's prophecy to Ourseau that when the emperor set foot in the Capitol his good fortune would be sleeping in his hand, and if it woke he would be safe but if it didn't he would die.

'Ah, Zephir, wise creature!' he said; and: 'Ah, false and treacherous Fortune!' And he mournfully reflected on the death of 'the flower and mirror of all chivalry, the valiant conqueror! What robbed you of your wisdom and discretion, always so unfailing, at the moment you were given this letter? It can only have been ill fortune, which diverted them while good fortune was sleeping in your hand.'

Caesar's men were now admitted, and they were horrified to see the senators gathered round the emperor's dead body.

'Sirs,' said Ursus, 'last night an ominous sign appeared in the city, and its meaning has proved dire indeed.' And he told them that the emperor had suddenly fallen dead before their eyes. 'I suggest he be carried to his palace while the nobles make arrangements for his burial.'

They did as Ursus said; and when those who'd received high honours and great riches from Caesar learned of his misfortune they were stricken with grief, but those who hated him or anticipated high station now that he was dead all rejoiced.

And that was how the death of Julius Caesar, the mighty emperor, was plotted.

The Adventure of the Red Sword

Britain, recovering from its destruction by the Romans, needs a new king and queen. The destined ones are King Gadifer's grandson Gallafur and Alexandre, 'the Maiden of the Dragons'. They are descendants not only of Perceforest and Gadifer but of Alexander, too, and their bloodline is to continue to one who will draw a sword that Gallafur has imbedded in a great stone: King Arthur himself. Arthur will thus have Greek blood, inherited from Alexander the Great. But, although the Maiden of the Dragons has captured Gallafur's heart, he is told that he will not be worthy of her – he will not even learn her name – unless he first achieves the Adventure of the Red Sword: he must carry the sword through the forest with its colour unchanged. This is destined to be accomplished by one of King Gadifer's line; but it is the test of true lovers, and three of Gallafur's kinsmen, Utran, Nero and Gadiforus, all fail in turn as each succumbs to the temptations of the alluring sisters Corsora, Canones and Carhaus: they consequently find the Red Sword turning black in their hands. Now it is Gallafur's turn. The test begins with the unhooking of the red sword from a pillar.

Gallafur rode to the pillar with all speed. But when confronted by the sword he was thrilled but also fearful of failure, very mindful that he would never be able to speak to the one he loved most in all the world until he'd achieved the adventure of the Red Sword. He was overjoyed when he took the sword, rose-red, from its hook with ease; and he set off with it through the forest, feeling that his life now depended on his success.

Shortly after noon he came to a glade surrounded by a dense body of hazel trees. The sun was shining after a spell of rain so the air was filled with a ravishing scent of flowers. Gallafur stopped to let his horse graze while he sat and refreshed his spirit in breathing the sweet fragrance. Suddenly, amid the hazel trees, he thought he heard four maidens in playful conversation; three were saying how much they wished their lovers were with them, and he heard a fourth say:

'Truly, Corsora, Canones and you, Carhaus, you've all good reason to wish they were here: it's clear from your swollen bellies that all three of you are with child! I wish Fortune would send to the forest a noble knight, descended from King Gadifer, so that I could be his lover and look forward to bearing fruit like you!'

Corsora replied to this youngest of the sisters, Capraise: 'I pray to the God of Maids' Desires that you won't have long to wait!'

At that moment they heard a horse whinny in the glade beyond the trees. Capraise was instantly filled with joy. Venus, who was at the heart of this, sent heat coursing through her limbs: she was sure that a knight of the good Maimed King's lineage[18] had unhooked the Red Sword – it only remained to fulfil the mystery's purpose. But being young as she was, Capraise felt nervous and shy, so the sisters sent one of their maids to find the knight.

The maid walked up to Gallafur as he sat there in the glade. Clearly, she said, he didn't have a sweetheart or he wouldn't be roaming the forest: 'True lovers don't wander away from their beloved!'

'It's true,' he replied, 'that the beauty I love isn't here, but I'm hers nonetheless wherever I may be, and always shall be as long as I live. Truly, damsel, do you think wandering knights are unfaithful? No, they go in search of adventures to improve themselves and enhance their honour.'

'The nearer you are to the fire, sir, the more you feel the heat, and the further you stray, the more you cool. So it is with love! And you surely know an absent pupil learns nothing new – indeed he forgets all he's learnt so far! Wandering knights are always in search of novelty! Their hearts are drawn to whatever chances to meet their eyes: they're like the swallow, catching his prey on the wing, first on one side, then on another!'

Not all were like that, Gallafur replied. Lyonnel du Glat had been a knight errant all his life but was renowned for having been most loyal in love. Le Tor de Pedrac had been constant in his love for Lyriope, young Gadifer faithful to his wife Flamine. And he himself, he said, was one such knight, and hungry now to achieve feats of prowess and make himself deserving of a maiden he loved with all his heart.

She asked him his name, and he said he called himself the Knight of the All-Surpassing Maiden, because the object of his love was the finest and most beautiful maiden in the kingdom.

'What brings you to this forest, then?'

'The adventure of the Red Sword,' he said, 'and if you know what I have to do to accomplish it, please tell me.'

---

[18] i.e. descended from King Gadifer, maimed by the boar.

'Well,' she replied, 'just close by are four sisters who can advise you better than anyone!' She told him to wait there while she found out if they were willing to help.

She returned to the sisters and told them she'd found a knight with the Red Sword, but he seemed very sure of his love for another maiden.

'In that case,' said Corsora, 'we shall have to use our wiles!' She sent the maid back to the glade to point Gallafur along a certain path.

So he rode through the hazel wood as she directed till he came to a grassy glade with a spring shaded by a linden tree. As he sheltered in the shadow of the woods he saw four maidens in beautiful attire, happily engaged in loosening the hair of the youngest, whose skin was snow-white, her cheeks red. When Gallafur saw this lovely girl, the sight of her blooming youth and perfect beauty made his body grow hot. But that doesn't surprise me: he was a man like any other. Now he was in a spot: Venus was setting her snares which, once you're caught, are very hard to escape! There was a great deal at stake here: if he betrayed and lost the Maiden of the Dragons, he would fail to have the wife prophesied by the Fairy Queen, and the one would not be born of his blood who would draw the sword from the Great Stone. But Gallafur had no thought of all this, so taken was he by the radiant beauty of the girl before him. They'd unlaced and removed one of her sleeves, and he heard one of the sisters say:

'Oh, we'd better surround her if we're going to undress her! Someone might be hiding in the woods and watching!'

So they gathered round their sister and stripped her naked, then wrapped her shift around her below the waist. But the valiant Gallafur, watching closely, saw the girl naked from the navel up. Nature had clearly taken care and pleasure in her making: her breasts were most appealing, as were her perfect neck and chin and face and yellow hair: I'm not surprised the knight was no longer master of himself! Then the sisters took her to bathe in the spring under the glorious shining sun.

'He'll be a lucky knight,' they said, 'who first enjoys love's pleasures with you!'

Then two of the sisters led her away to lie down and keep warm – but Gallafur didn't know where. Corsora and their maids were still at the spring, so he rode down and asked if they were the ones who could advise him about the adventure of the Red Sword.

'The knight who achieves it,' Corsora told him, 'will have to be exceptional: he'll need to earn the love of the goddess Venus, who holds the key to this adventure. A number of knights have failed because their behaviour didn't please the goddess at all. It's her will you must seek to follow, or you're wasting your time!'

'Damsel,' Gallafur replied, 'I'm only too eager to serve the goddess Venus, as long as it doesn't jeopardise the honour of the one to whom I've given my love.'

Corsora was very troubled by this. 'That's not a good start!' she said. 'It won't help you achieve what you desire if you're going to suspect the goddess's motives! That's offensive to the ancient gods who took Venus into their paradise and made her goddess of love; and from the very beginning Venus has had such power that anything done with her blessing is sure to be beyond reproach: to suspect her of wrongdoing is against nature! I assure you, sir, the goddess commands that the joys of love-making should be free of constraint – she takes any blame upon herself! If you want to achieve this adventure, bear that in mind!'

So saying, she told him to follow the course of the stream from the spring. 'And if you're offered lodging at the house ahead, don't decline, for the ones who live there are so much in favour with the goddess Venus that she often goes there to take her ease and pleasure!'

Gallafur duly set out, but Corsora overtook him by another path and reached the house of her sister Capraise before him; and there they prepared to make Gallafur unfaithful in the hope that Capraise would bear fruit of noble stock.

When Gallafur arrived he was greeted by two maids who instantly offered him lodging. 'The maiden who is mistress of the house,' they said, 'will be delighted to welcome you: the goddess Venus is due to be here tonight and the maiden wouldn't want to be alone, without the company of a knight, when such a potent goddess is expected as a guest!'

'It's a great honour,' he said, 'to be asked to entertain such a noble lady as the goddess Venus, and I've never seen her before as far as I recall!'

They thanked him, and promised he would gain much from pleasing the goddess and his hostess.

'I wish to do nothing less,' he said, 'saving the honour and the peace of the one I love.'

They were surprised, they said, to hear him make such a qualification, since everything in matters of love was in the gift of the goddess, and 'there can be no falsehood or betrayal in fulfilling her wishes.'

They led Gallafur to the hall, so sumptuous, so filled with sweet fragrance, that it was like entering a paradise, and lit in such a perfect way that it might well have been deemed a place for lovers. Gallafur said it was worthy to receive King Perceforest.

'It's a noble place indeed,' said one of the maids, 'but it's nothing compared with the chamber prepared for the goddess Venus! You'll be able to see it for yourself before the night is out!'

He was helped from his armour and clad in a rich mantle. Then they asked him if he desired anything while he was waiting for his hostess; he asked merely for her name.

'Sir,' said one of the maids, 'her name is Capraise. She's one of four noble sisters who live in this forest; and it's hoped that from one of them will descend the king who's to bring Britain greater glory than it has ever known: blessed be the father of the line!'

At that moment three maidens of the utmost beauty appeared from a chamber. One of them was Corsora, who welcomed Gallafur warmly 'on behalf of the mistress of the house and the three of us who are her sisters. We were in want of a worthy knight to pay honour to the goddess Venus and keep her company! And that's not all: the goddess knows that from one of us four sisters will descend the most renowned king who ever was and ever will be born in Britain. To ensure this, the goddess Venus has so contrived it that no living knight can take the Red Sword from its hook unless he's worthy of begetting such an heir. Blessed be the body of the one who yields such seed! Fortunate indeed will be the one who bears the Red Sword through the forest with its colour unchanged, a task which none has yet achieved because they failed to do the goddess's will.' This was known, said Corsora, by a number of noble maidens, who considered the accomplishment of the adventure so important that they desired no other lover than the knight who achieved it. 'Several have told knights they favour not to return to them or aspire to their love until they've accomplished this adventure. But the one who succeeds will be most fortunate, for such a maiden then will deny him nothing! And the gods will smile on him and all his line!'

Gallafur thought instantly of his beloved Maiden of the Dragons. He was close to falling into Corsora's trap, seized as he was by the will to do whatever the goddess Venus now commanded – the more so as he remembered what he'd been told earlier that day: that the noble goddess could absolve him from any wrong.

Corsora saw him flushing with excitement and asked him: 'What are you thinking, sir?'

'About the adventure of the Red Sword,' he replied. 'If I fail, I'll never know the name or station of the one I love most in all the world.'

'What a stroke of luck, then, sir!' she said. 'For if you do the goddess's bidding tonight I've no doubt you'll accomplish the adventure and carry back the Red Sword to your love!'

'Damsel,' said Gallafur, 'I greatly desire to do Venus's bidding, saving always the honour and the peace of the one I love.'

When Corsora heard these words she was very disturbed and said: 'Sir knight, you're not likely to please the goddess if you put yourself in other hands than hers. Just when she most expects to have pleasure and service from you, another might intervene and forbid it! Then she, presiding as she does over this adventure, would send you from the forest with the Red Sword black as ink, and you'd be robbed of the one you love most in all the world and banished from her forever!'

Gallafur was horrified; he was shaking with fear. 'Tell me,' he said, 'if tonight I failed to do her bidding out of ignorance, would there be any second chance?'

'Well,' Corsora replied, 'this is one of three houses in the forest haunted by the goddess Venus, and if she fails to have satisfaction here she might bear it graciously and go to the second house tomorrow night. If she fails to be satisfied there she will doubtless be most displeased; and if at the third house – where she expects the greatest pleasure! – she is again left unsatisfied by the service she receives, then all will be lost, and she'll return to her paradise and leave the knight who's failed her high and dry!'

Gallafur was cheered to know he'd have more than one chance, and said: 'I shall happily await whatever lies in store in the hope of achieving the adventure.'

'Well said, sir!' Corsora replied. 'And I promise to do all I can to help you!'

With that she led him to the most luxurious chamber he'd ever seen. At one side stood a table with a sumptuous spread of food and drink, at the head of which sat a young maiden so beautiful and so richly adorned that Gallafur took her to be the goddess Venus! He went down on his knees! She bade him welcome and invited him to 'open your heart to joy, for this is a chamber devoted to pleasure and delight and the fulfilment of all amorous desires!'

Still thinking she was the goddess, Gallafur promised to cast off all cares, for 'you are the lady whom all lovers should serve and honour!'

She thanked him and bade him sit at her side, while each of her three sisters chose one of three other young knights who were there in the chamber and took him to sit with her at the table. The maiden who Gallafur thought was Venus asked him his name and lineage, and he told her his father was Gadifer, son of the Maimed King and the Fairy Queen, and his mother was Flamine, daughter of Aroés of the Sheer Mountain; his name was Gallafur, he said, and he was their eldest son. Hearing this, and seeing his strong and appealing body, she flushed with love, thinking that he more than any man alive should beget the line that would lead to the prophesied king, and she would be the most fortunate girl in the world if she could bear his child.

'But I wouldn't have told you my name,' he said, 'if you hadn't been the goddess Venus!'

Hearing this, she smiled and said: 'I can help you in your adventure: without my blessing neither you nor any other can achieve it.'

And he, convinced of her divine omniscience, said: 'Let me tell you the truth that you already know!' And he told her how he yearned to accomplish the adventure because of his love for the Maiden of the Dragons, 'and if I fail I wish for nothing but death – I'd rather die than live without hope of her!'

The girl was less than pleased by this: she was as stricken with love for him as he was for the Maiden of the Dragons. But she knew that, deluded as he was into thinking her the goddess, she had every chance of working her wiles upon him. She claimed she was very fond of the Maiden of the Dragons, which was why she'd told her about the adventure of the Red Sword and encouraged her to set the challenge before any knight she loved. 'So the fact that she told you

suggests she truly loves you! Trust me, you can do whatever you desire in this house tonight: it is my will that you should, and the goddess's will should be obeyed!'

'Dear lady,' said Gallafur, 'I greatly desire to do everything to please
you – saving always the honour and the peace of the one I love.'

The girl was enraged by these words, but hid her anger and replied: 'That's well said, sir! But if you truly knew me you wouldn't put
any obstacle in the way of my desires! If I'm displeased, you know,
I'm quite capable of cloaking myself in my wintry mantle and leaving wretches frozen and deprived of comfort, scouring the forests in
vain for help and solace! If you fail to please me, you'll return to your
land bereft of any honour from this adventure and banished from
the Maiden of the Dragons!' Seeing his alarm, she soothed him then
with sweet words: 'Have no fears about serving the goddess: her only
concern is joy! Nothing she desires can be displeasing to a man – and
you don't look like a man with cause to doubt his ability to serve her!
And in this house all delights and pleasures are as secret as if they'd
never happened!'

What a fool he was being, he told himself! All that was required
of him was to indulge in pleasure that night and he'd achieve his
quest! And when he voiced these thoughts aloud, the whole company
plunged into a rapturous mood, and Gallafur thought of nothing but
joy in the here and now. The one he loved so much was quite forgotten; his sole intent was to please the girl Capraise, who he thought
was the goddess Venus. She made sure he was copiously served at
supper, especially with exquisite spiced drinks, guaranteed to fire the
blood and incline the heart to pleasure.

The company was in an ecstatic mood by the time supper was over,
whereupon Capraise summoned them all to gather the next night 'at a
house I call the Second Pleasure. You are especially invited, sir knight:
I want us to have even more fun there!'

And with that she left the chamber. Gallafur, seeing her go, said
to Carhaus, seated beside him: 'I'm very sorry I didn't ask the goddess what I have to do now regarding my quest – I seem to be in her
favour, I'm pleased to say!'

Carhaus told him not to worry: he should just enjoy himself, and
'if she seeks your company tonight or at some other time – she comes
and goes invisibly, turning up in surprising places! – and she wants

something from you, do as she wishes. If you do, you can't fail to achieve your quest!'

The merriment continued far into the night. Then the company departed, leaving Gallafur alone. But soon a maid came and led him to another chamber, where he found a bed fit for a prince; and she said:

'Sir, lie down in this bed. I promise you, if you do what's required of you here, you'll have little or nothing left to do to achieve the adventure of the Red Sword.'

He asked her what he was supposed to do.

'I can't believe,' she replied, 'that Nature hasn't told you! Dumb beasts, unendowed with reason, know! Just lie there comfortably and all will be revealed!'

And she left the chamber and shut the door fast. Gallafur was in the goddess Venus's prison! But what a sweet imprisonment it was! For there in the gorgeous bed lay a soft and white-skinned girl in the first flush of youth, her lovely face coloured by Nature under the goddess Venus's guidance. She was quite naked, and the knight, being in the flower of youth himself, was so seized by burning desire that he didn't know what was happening to him. And Nature surged within him and equipped him with the strong, hard wherewithal to fulfil his desire. Nothing was going to stop him lying naked beside that beauty.

While he stripped, she, feigning sleep, gave a sigh – of desire more than trepidation. She had quite overcome any fear or sense of shame – daring and youthful passion prevailed. Gallafur heard the sigh and turned and saw her lovely face and couldn't wait to kiss it and be beside her. But at the moment of the kiss he chanced to think of the Maiden of the Dragons for whom he'd been yearning so much; he stopped in his tracks, wondering what he was doing. When Nature, who had fired him to such a mighty pitch, saw this, She instantly withdrew all that She'd lent and hid in a corner, shame-faced and crestfallen, leaving Gallafur, like one half-dead, propped on his elbows with his head in his hands. He'd lost all sense of where he was, and high up on the chamber wall he saw a vision of the Maiden of the Dragons, furiously telling her chambermaid:

'Now you see the knight's falseness! Any woman who shows her heart to a man before she's put him to the test is a fool! I should never have bothered telling him about the adventure of the Red Sword! But

I did so with good intentions – I thought he was the true and valiant stock that would bring all honour to the kingdom.'

But the chambermaid replied: 'He hasn't yet done anything that can't be quickly pardoned: he hasn't given way to a sin that would bar him from achieving the adventure. From his manner I'd say he repents of his wicked intent.'

'Be that as it may,' said the Maiden of the Dragons, 'he'll never be forgiven until he's been truly shamed!'

This shocked Gallafur out of his fantasy – when he looked again he saw only the wall. He realised he'd been tricked by the urgings of the goddess Venus, and the maidens had been trying to deceive him. From now on he'd know how to avoid their wiles.

But just as he was berating himself for his foolishness he heard a voice say: 'What do you think of this knight?'

And another voice replied: 'He's not worthy to be in the ladies' chamber or to accomplish the adventure of the Red Sword. Throw him out!'

And a moment later he felt himself being grabbed from all sides and hauled from the chamber – and suddenly he was in the middle of the forest beside his horse with all his gear lying in the grass.

He sat there, bewildered by all that had happened, till daybreak. What was he to think? On the one hand Love told him he couldn't achieve the adventure unless he was faithful to the maiden he loved with all his heart, but on the other the maidens who claimed to be in control of the adventure 'said it wouldn't be achieved by any man unless he fulfilled their desires – which seem entirely opposed to faithfulness!' He felt he surely couldn't win: he was bound to lose the one he loved. But since it was so, 'it's better to have people say "there goes the knight who lost his lady through loyalty" than "through base lust"! I hope that choosing to do good will be rewarded some time, so I'll stick to the decent way.'

All that day he rode without direction, until he found himself back at the stream from the spring he'd visited the evening before. He was relieved – both he and his horse were very thirsty. He drank and sat down at the edge of a spinney and set his horse free to graze. And as he sat there, deep in thought about his adventure, a girl saw him and guessed he was the knight that the maiden Capraise had sent her to find. She sat quietly nearby and heard him say to himself:

'This adventure should be called the test of true lovers – and it's a good and useful one for all ladies and maidens who are in love or wish to be: a woman is sorely deceived if she gives her heart to a faithless man.'

Hearing this, the girl decided to heap praise on him for his words – just as the devil, seeing someone too committed to good deeds to be led astray by wicked urgings, cunningly makes him so conscious of his own goodness that it turns to vain self-righteousness. The girl saw this was the best way to trick the knight, so she spoke up, approving his words most fulsomely and telling him:

'All who undergo this test and remain true to their ladies will be deemed faithful lovers, and the more they're tested with temptations the more they'll esteemed and honoured! I've never seen a man as committed to loyalty as you: you, I'm sure, can resist all the temptations offered by the maidens who control this adventure. And if you succeed, the goddess Venus will be delighted and her wishes fulfilled, despite all appearances to the contrary: for otherwise, how could any knight emerge from this adventure a winner?'

Gallafur thanked her warmly, and proudly declared: 'My heart is so steadfast, and the one I love so glorious, that I shan't avoid their temptations, but earn more credit by facing them and resisting them all!'

'I commend you to God!' she said, and left him, saying: 'Mount and ride, sir – adventure will soon come your way!'

So he followed the line of the stream, cheered and excited by what the girl had said; and he drew the sword to check its colour and found it as red as ever. With darkness falling he met another girl who invited him to take lodging nearby where 'the mistress of the house is in want of company to entertain a lady who's come to visit her.' And so it was that Gallafur was taken to the same house and the very same chamber as the night before – but he didn't recognise them: all was entirely new to him. Once again he was given a glorious welcome and presented with a sumptuous spread. And again a maiden of exceeding beauty appeared, and he was sure she was the goddess Venus – but of course it was Capraise.

'Welcome, sir,' she said, 'though I don't believe you'd have come here if I hadn't sent for you, despite my invitation last night!'

'My lady,' Gallafur replied, 'as your true knight I'm ready to make amends for any wrongs.'

'That's good enough for me!' she said. And with that, they took their places at the table with other knights and maidens and joyous feasting began.

'Sir,' she said, 'I hope you'll be merrier at supper than you were last night: you were very drowsy by the time we went to bed.' And she continued, teasingly: 'It's a good idea to know how to please women! A man who serves them without giving full satisfaction loses all praise and reward. There'll be no excuse – they like their desires properly fulfilled!'

'He's a lucky man who manages that!' said Gallafur. 'I don't think there's a man alive who can! If he pleases one there'll be another who'll never forgive him! That's why they just seek to please the ones they love most.'

'Men shouldn't worry,' she replied. 'A man who can serve and please one maiden is likely to satisfy all others!'

Capraise should be forgiven for trying to lead Gallafur astray: it was principally for the honour of bearing the prophesied king, not so much for the pleasure of love-making – though she wasn't averse to the pleasure, either! But the chastest of the country's maidens would have desired that honour. As it was, not knowing which of Gadifer's line was destined to father that illustrious descendant, three of the four sisters were already with child by three noble knights of Gadifer's blood, and the fourth was working hard to join them: as they ate, Capraise spoke many amorous words to the noble Gallafur and plied him with spiced drinks to attract him to her and make him forget his other love. By the end of supper he looked more aroused and excited than she'd ever seen him. She took her leave then, whereupon everyone retired to bed; and a maid took Gallafur by the hand and left him in a beautiful, softly-lit chamber with a bed ready-made.

He undressed and lay down naked in the bed. And I tell you, once he'd slipped beneath the sheets he could feel the body of a girl, young, tender and fit! She, feigning sleep, gave a little breath and stretched her arms above the coverlet to reveal her face and her nakedness, right down to the middle of her firm, pert breasts. Gallafur's body was afire, and Nature supplied him with the weapon he needed to conquer the castle; and Venus came to the bed, swiftly and unseen, and did all in her power to spur them both with amorous desires. Gallafur now felt he should wake the girl, for he thought it shameful and treacherous to assail her as she slept, but he needn't have worried: in this instance the lady of the castle was inviting attack, spreading her arms wide to the knight while feigning deepest sleep. All Gallafur's forces were raring to go, hungry for booty. But at that very moment, with the delectable prospect right before him, Love stepped between and confronted him with his falseness and betrayal of the best and most beautiful maiden of all, and with the disastrous consequences of going through with the attack: this wasn't the action of a loyal knight, and he should give up this fleeting pleasure for a greater honour and a lasting joy. It was all over; Nature called to her forces to put down their weapons – their lord had a weak and cowardly heart and they had no chance of victory here!

His fever gone, aware now of how close he'd been to danger, Gallafur slipped quietly from the bed, not wanting to wake the one who wasn't sleeping, and dressed again. A moment later the light went out, and he was seized and hauled from the chamber amid cries of 'Cowardly knight, be gone from here!' And once again he found himself in the middle of the forest with his horse and his arms and the Red Sword hanging from his saddle.

All next day he rode, and when evening came he found himself once more beside the stream from the spring. Again he drank and sat and reflected on what had happened. He feared he'd failed in the adventure, but feared still more that in achieving it he'd lose the one he loved most in all the world; for as far as he could see, the maidens were bent on making him commit a sin involving undeniable falseness and betrayal. He declared aloud his commitment to utter loyalty, even if it condemned him to defeat.

His words were overheard by the girl who'd met him there the day before, and she came forward now and said: 'If you'd believed what I told you this time yesterday, you wouldn't be giving up hope like this! The goddess Venus is so kind and compassionate in matters of love that your loyalty won't cost you success in the adventure. Carry on! I promise you, if you're brave enough to go and face it, no nobler adventure ever befell any man as will befall you tonight – and none ever so pleased a man as this one will please you! If you've the courage to seize this chance, before tomorrow dawns all your trials and efforts will be rewarded!'

'Damsel,' Gallafur replied, 'the joy you promise can come to me only from the beauty who's won my heart.'

'Oh sir, if you love a maiden so well, tonight your joy will be complete, for the goddess Venus, I promise you, means to repay the loyalty she's seen in you so richly that you couldn't ask for more!'

With that she was gone, and Gallafur set out again, following the line of the stream. Still dreading failure, he checked the sword's colour once more – and hope returned to his heart when he found it still as red as any rose.

Suddenly a girl appeared and invited him to a house known as the Third Pleasure, to which 'the goddess Venus has summoned a maiden from the kingdom of England. She's very dear to her, and she's called her to her house of delight to see a knight accomplish the adventure! The maiden's now arrived, and she's so beautiful and noble and witty and wise that I'd say she's all-surpassing!'

Into the house Gallafur followed the girl, his heart racing. 'What?' he said to himself. 'Could it really be the Maiden of the Dragons?'

She led him to a hall filled with a joyous company of ladies and knights and maidens. Then the door of a chamber opened and two boys appeared bearing torches which blazed with a flame of such a nature that Gallafur's perceptions were wholly altered: behind them came two maidens hand in hand, more beautiful and more exquisitely attired than any he'd ever seen; and one, he believed, was the goddess Venus and the other he was convinced was the Maiden of the Dragons. He was so overwhelmed by his love for her that he couldn't speak or bow. The maiden he thought was the goddess, seeing him so spellbound, knew it was because of his deluded view of her companion. She let go of her sister's hand – for the maiden was really her sister – and came to Gallafur and said:

'Sir knight, celebrate as you've never done in your life! Before morning I'll unite you with the one you love most in all the world – and who loves you in return, I know. And because I've found you to be the most loyal of all knights, and so that you may fulfil what she's demanded of you, I grant you success in the challenge of the Red Sword: you may confidently go from the forest with the sword's colour unchanged!'

Gallafur was overcome with joy and said: 'Lady, goddess of true lovers, I place my soul and my body in your hands, to do with them as you please.'

'Well said, sir!' said the maiden. And she turned to her sister

Capraise and whispered: 'Our spell is working well! The knight thinks you're the one he calls the Maiden of the Dragons, whom he loves so truly that he can't be led astray. But if he escapes this time I'll never value women's wiles again!'

She took Capraise and Gallafur and seated them on either side of her as the joyous feast began. Gallafur was in a state of wonder, never having thought he'd be so close to his beloved until he'd accomplished the adventure she'd demanded of him. Then the goddess – who that night was really Corsora – sent a squire to fetch the Red Sword and presented it to Gallafur, saying:

'Take this sword, sir knight, with its colour untainted, for you are worthy to succeed in this adventure. And by achieving it you will take to wife the most beautiful and high-born maiden in the land: the one you've loved so long. And a further honour will come to you: this very night the two of you will beget a child from whom will descend an heir so valiant and devoted to chivalry that the gods have ordained he'll draw the sword you buried in the stone. And since you've proved yourself worthy of all this, I wish you now to marry this maiden, to honour her and your noble line to come!'

When Gallafur heard these words from Corsora – who he thought was Venus – he was filled with joy, and bowed to her and said there was nothing he desired more in all the world; and Capraise – who he thought was the Maiden of the Dragons – thanked her sister deeply for granting her this honour and said:

'Such are your power and might that I wouldn't dare disobey!'

Then Corsora joined their hands together and appealed to all the company to celebrate their noble marriage. And the sisters rejoiced indeed: Capraise was about to be coupled with the eldest son of the eldest son of the Maimed King Gadifer, and although they would rather have been with child by him than by the three knights they'd managed to deceive, they were delighted that their youngest sister was now set fair.

Soon it was time for them to take the bride to bed; then Corsora, the supposed goddess, came to Gallafur and said: 'Now we'll take you to the bridal chamber: the time has come! Be sure to conduct yourself properly! Let her have no cause for complaint!'

'Thank you, lady! I wouldn't be so happy if I'd won all the gold in the world!'

And he stepped into the chamber, rejoicing at his good fortune, and closed the door behind him. And he turned to the bed, the richest and most luxurious he'd ever beheld, and saw a maiden lying there, her face tucked under the whitest of coverlets.

'Ah God!' he whispered then. 'How can it be that you've earned such reward at so little cost?' It suddenly dawned on him that he hadn't yet carried the Red Sword from the forest with its colour unchanged. 'Might I not,' he asked himself, 'earn lifelong reproach and be accused of stealing another man's honour if I took the prize now at women's bidding rather than through my own prowess? And even if the one I love so much has granted me her favour at the request of the goddess Venus, I must keep my word! And guard her honour and mine as a true lover should!'

Gallafur sat on the edge of the bed and said, very gently: 'My beautiful, dearest love, please listen to me now. Since I first saw you at the Great Stone, when you gave me the sword and I cut the dragons' chains, I've been utterly in love with you. I've set my heart upon achieving the adventures you've required of me, and now I find myself married to you before I've accomplished anything! How can this be right? I'd rather have you angry with me for this present moment than rush into something that would bring you shame hereafter and cause you deep regret. Tell me what you want to do: my wish is to preserve your honour and mine by waiting till I've achieved these adventures according to the original terms.'

Capraise, desperately impatient, said: 'I haven't come here to engage in debate! It's hardly the time! This is the hour for pleasure and rest! Morning will come soon enough, and then we can discuss such matters: forget them for now!'

But Gallafur was deeply uneasy and wouldn't give way. 'I'll not rest,' he declared, 'until I've accomplished what you demanded of me!' And so saying he donned his armour and, with the Red Sword at his waist, strode angrily to the chamber door.

Capraise went wild and started screaming: 'Seize this useless knight and take the Red Sword! He's not worthy to achieve the adventure!'

Gallafur was grabbed from every side and hauled from the chamber and dumped in the forest amid cries of: 'Cowardly wretch! What's wrong with you? You'd better watch out! Before you leave the forest the Red Sword will be seized from you!'

Gallafur was left there, bewildered, in the starlight: there was no one to be seen. But he found his horse saddled and ready, and a lance beside him, much to his delight: he vowed he'd defend the Red Sword to the death. He was determined to complete the adventure by force of arms, finding it hard to believe that the Maiden of the Dragons would wish it otherwise.

He rode for a while but, having not slept that night, he dismounted then and lay down to rest on the dewy grass until the warming sun appeared. Then he rose and set out again. But he'd gone no distance before three heavily armed knights blocked his way and cried:

'Lay down the Red Sword, you feeble wretch! It doesn't belong to you! We've been sent to take it back to its hook to await the valiant knight who's to achieve the adventure.'

'Truly, sirs,' Gallafur replied, 'I'm not such a wretch or so feeble as to lay down the sword because of your threats. If you want it you'll have to win it by the strength of your arms and the blades of your swords!'

The first knight charged and shattered his lance as he smashed through Gallafur's shield; but Gallafur unhorsed him with a grievous wound to the shoulder. He toppled the second knight, too; but the third kept his saddle as both their lances flew into splinters. They drew their swords and exchanged fearsome blows. Gallafur was soon on the point of victory, but the second knight remounted and came to his companion's aid and smashed Gallafur's shield to pieces. Gallafur responded with a blow that severed the knight's arm and put him to flight. The third was too exhausted to fight longer and said:

'Pass on if you wish, sir knight: I'll not bar your way!'

'You'll not escape that easily,' said Gallafur. 'Tell me who told you to guard this passage or I'll take the life from your body.'

The knight refused to say – it was expressly forbidden; but when Gallafur raised his sword to kill him he confessed: it was the four sisters who had sent them 'to kill you or at least to take the Red Sword'.

'Tell me,' said Gallafur, 'is one of them the goddess Venus?'

'Certainly not!' the knight replied. 'It's all part of their enchantment, to make you have carnal knowledge of their youngest sister, for their divinations have revealed the great descendant who's to be born of Gadifer's line. They established this adventure of the Red Sword to attract knights of Gadifer's blood; the three older sisters are already with child by them, and the fourth expected to be this time! It was because of her rage at having failed that she bade us confront you and seize the Red Sword or put you to death. We've clearly failed!'

Filled with joy that it had all been an enchantment, Gallafur sent the knight on his way, and then rode along the path and out of the forest. As soon as he was in open country he drew the Red Sword to see if it had kept its colour – and yes! He found it, indeed, even redder than before! He was jubilant: he had truly accomplished the adventure.

But a moment later an old man appeared and demanded the sword: he would return it to the pillar. 'That's where it belongs; in any case, you've turned it black.'

'I don't think I have, good sir,' said Gallafur. 'Here it is, as red as it was before I took it from the hook.'

And he showed him the sword, ruby-red, and the old man was astonished. 'Truly, sir knight,' he said, 'it seems you've achieved the adventure in which a good many worthy knights have failed.' And bidding him 'take the sword where you will', he promptly vanished.

And Gallafur set out for England to find news of the Maiden of the Dragons.

Printed and bound by CPI Group (UK) Ltd, Croydon, CR0 4YY

14/04/2025